# THE TREASURES
# OF CHILDHOOD

# THE TREASURES OF CHILDHOOD

## BOOKS, TOYS, AND GAMES FROM THE OPIE COLLECTION

Iona and Robert Opie and Brian Alderson

PAVILION

This edition published in Great Britain in 1995 by
PAVILION BOOKS LIMITED
26 Upper Ground, London SE1 9PD

Originally published in hardback in 1989

Introduction and Books Section text copyright © Brian Alderson 1989
Toys Section text copyright © Iona and Robert Opie 1989
Books copyright © The Bodleian Library, Oxford 1989
Toys and Games Collection copyright © Iona Opie 1989

Designed by Christos Kondeatis
Jacket designed by Bernard Higton
Cover photograph by Angelo Hornak

A CIP catalogue record for this book is available from the
British Library

ISBN 1 85793 624 8

Printed and bound in Spain

2 4 6 8 10 9 7 5 3 1

This book may be ordered by post direct from the publisher.
Please contact the Marketing Department.
But try your bookshop first.

# CONTENTS

# PREFACE

espite the lure of video machines and computer games, children are still to be found preoccupied with the rituals of jumping over a turning rope or wheeling a doll's pram down imaginary avenues; and despite a preponderance of electronic thrills they may still be tucked into bed to the lilt of a nursery rhyme or the rhythms of a fairy-tale. Nor is it yet beyond belief that these experiences will so root themselves in the child's mind that, like 'Rosebud' for Citizen Kane, they will dwell there through all the vicissitudes of the future.

But while it is easy to be sentimental about these customary pleasures, a precise knowledge of their origins and evolution is not so readily achieved. What genius invented skipping games, and who first manufactured ropes with handles attached so that they might be more easily played? Where do nursery rhymes come from, and what – if anything – do they mean?

Questions of this kind caught the imagination of Iona and Peter Opie early on in their married life, and for nearly forty years they pursued the answers through the murky byways of folklore and bibliography, printed sources and oral history. With the publication of their *Oxford Dictionary of Nursery Rhymes* in 1951 they set an entirely new standard for the study of the literature of childhood – so often dismissed as jejune or trivial – and in a succession of books that followed, and through their participation in the work of the Folklore Society (of which Peter was President in 1963–4) they steadily extended our knowledge of the rituals and customs that have been inherited by, or imposed upon, the young.

In the course of this work, and as a necessary adjunct to it, they gradually assembled a mighty collection of books and other objects which gave imaginative access to the past lives that they were studying. At the centre of the Collection were some twenty thousand children's books – many of great rarity – together with a host of related ephemera such as painting-books and 'penny-dreadfuls'; and alongside these was a massive representation of the toys, games and other pastimes that have been contrived to keep children happy (or to yield profitable returns to their producers). Evangelical tales about gutter-snipes could be lined up alongside elaborate German pop-up books, lace dresses for dolls were stored not far from whoopee-cushions.

For many years Iona and Peter Opie nurtured a hope that the whole Collection might form an independent 'museum of childhood' to complement those already established in such places as London and Edinburgh. The financial and administrative complexities of the plan were excessive, however, and, after Peter's death in 1982, Iona resolved to divide the books from the rest of the Collection and to seek a home for them in the Bodleian Library at Oxford. (Both she and Peter had felt strong affinities for the place, for not only were most of their books published by the University's Clarendon Press, but much of their early work on the *Dictionary of Nursery Rhymes* had been done in the Bodleian Library itself.)

Following this decision, the Opie Collection of Children's Literature was subjected to a detailed appraisal and was offered to Bodley at half its valuation – which had reached the neatly rounded figure of one million pounds. An appeal was launched under the patronage of the Prince of Wales and in May 1988 the sponsors were able to announce that the money had been raised. The books were transferred to Oxford, where an Endowment Trust has been established to help finance cataloguing and to enable the Collection to be extended. The toys, games and other trappings of childhood remain in the possession of Iona Opie.

This illustrated survey of what was once known as the Opie Collection of Child Life and Literature was planned in the early stages of the Appeal and was intended primarily as a celebration of the Opie ideal of making a representative survey of all the facets of the history of childhood; and in the course of such a description it is only natural that we should record and portray some of the outstanding features of the Collection as it existed at Westerfield House. We may not perhaps reveal the Full True History of skipping-ropes or nursery songs, but we have tried to show how, through work on the Collection, that history may be more completely traced and understood.

All royalties from *The Treasures of Childhood* will be donated to the Endowment Fund at the Bodleian Library with high hopes that the arrival of the Collection will be a stimulus to the more fruitful study of children's literature.

*Iona Opie*
*Robert Opie*
*Brian Alderson*

At Westerfield House
*c.* 1960, soon after Iona and
Peter Opie had moved in.

# INTRODUCTION

## OVER THE HILLS TO WEST LISS

he rolling English road that takes you from Farnham in Surrey to Petersfield in Hampshire is a fair example of the highway-planning undertaken by Chesterton's rolling English drunkard. In the course of its reeling progress it eventually gets to the village of West Liss, and there, within the crook of one of its more dramatic bends – in between 'The Spread Eagle' and 'The Blue Bell' – lies Westerfield House where for so long the Opie Collection grew and flourished. 'We've always lived next door to a pub,' says Iona Opie nostalgically, as though to contrast the cheerful informality that goes with the splendid beer of Hampshire and the more austere excitements of creating and exploiting a collection.

Westerfield is by no means an elegant mansion – a late Victorian farmhouse, built rather like a Victorian rectory, and likened by Iona and Peter Opie, from time to time, to a couple of Noah's arks joined along the sides. And that is not an inappropriate image. For by associating Westerfield House with ideas of rescue and preservation – to say nothing of Sunday playtime in the Victorian nursery – one derives a sense of the 'treasures of childhood' saved from a neglectful public and herded into those angular, red-brick walls.

All the evidence suggests that the Collection was pre-ordained, that it couldn't help but happen. Before they ever knew each other Iona and Peter Opie were people who collected things (mostly books), and after they met and married there was contented agreement that collecting was a nice thing to do – with no guilty smuggling of irresistible bargains into hidden corners for fear

Westerfield House – the two Noah's arks: a view from the air.

of reprisals. What was lacking was a focus, a defined area where collected artefacts might achieve a richer significance through their relationships one with another.

That focus came in 1945, soon after Iona and Peter Opie had begun work on the book that was to make their names, the *Oxford Dictionary of Nursery Rhymes*. Like many a master-work it had started in an almost offhand way through curiosity over what might be the origin and significance of that heroic poem 'Ladybird, ladybird, fly away home', and from that initial prompting came the thought – both daunting and stimulating – of all those other rhymes that everyone takes for granted. How many of them were there? Where did they come from? Was it possible to discriminate between the authenticity of variant versions? (As the *Dictionary* eventually showed, for instance, care for ladybirds and rhymes about them occur all over the world; it also notes that the first English version of the rhyme, *c.*1744, said 'your children will burn' rather than 'your children are gone', and that the second stanza about little Ann creeping under the pan did not get into print for another hundred years.)

At the start of their research the Opies worked from borrowed copies of such preliminary sources as James Orchard Halliwell's *Nursery Rhymes of England*, first published in 1842, and they followed up leads from there by delving among the books in the national collection at the British Museum. Then one day Peter Opie arrived home from his job at a publishing house with a glint of revelation in his eye. He had happened to pass Hatchard's bookshop in Piccadilly, had gone in to look around, and had there bought a flimsy, paper-covered booklet of nursery rhymes called *The Cheerful Warbler*: sixteen pages, illustrated with little woodcuts and published at a price of One Penny by the York bookseller James Kendrew round about 1820. Nothing about it was impressive. The rhymes were a random bunch; the cuts were ugly, and clearly part of a much-used stock; but by its very unimpressiveness *The Cheerful Warbler* gave token of how widely and deeply nursery rhymes had penetrated the world of print and had become part of the accepted culture of the nation. If James Kendrew could offer a pennyworth of ditties for cheerful warbling in 1820, how much more evidence might be lying around in neglected books and chapbooks? What might be discovered of the interrelationship of versions and variants if all the printed sources could be assembled and compared? The thrill of what might be entailed in answering those questions gave the first impetus to the making of the Opie Collection.

As Iona recalls it, the Collection – once started – played a decisive part in

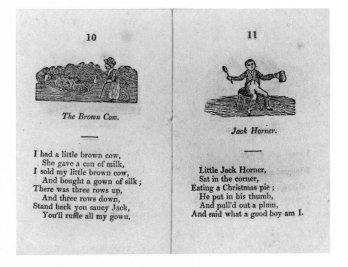

The Brown Cow.

I had a little brown cow,
  She gave a can of milk,
I sold my little brown cow,
  And bought a gown of silk;
There was three rows up,
  And three rows down,
Stand back you saucy Jack,
  You'll ruffle all my gown.

Jack Horner.

Little Jack Horner,
Sat in the corner,
Eating a Christmas pie;
  He put in his thumb,
  And pull'd out a plum,
And said what a good boy am I.

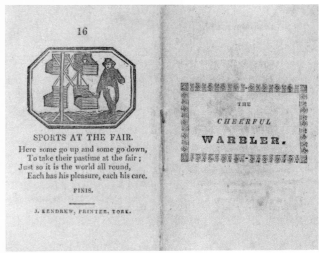

SPORTS AT THE FAIR.

Here some go up and some go down,
  To take their pastime at the fair;
Just so it is the world all round,
  Each has his pleasure, each his care.

FINIS.

J. KENDREW, PRINTER, YORK.

*The Cheerful Warbler, or juvenile song book.* York: printed and sold by J. Kendrew, n.d. [*c.*1820]. 97×65 mm.

Cover and final page (coloured yellow in the original), with two intermediate pages. The 'Sports at the Fair' cut was also used by Kendrew in his alphabet book *The Silver Penny* to illustrate 'U' for 'Up-and-Down'.

Ten examples of chapbooks published by Kendrew of York round about the same time that he issued *The Cheerful Warbler*. They have been chosen as a cross-section of the topics that he hoped would do well in the market-place:

*We Are Seven* is an attempt to convert Wordsworth's poem into a popular commodity (something that the poet himself hoped might one day happen).

*Mrs. Lovechild's Golden Present* is an alphabet and syllabary with a distinctively eighteenth-century flavour, which also goes for the stories and moral padding in *Tom Thumb's Folio, The Foundling* and *Giles Gingerbread*.

Also represented are traditional fare: *Fables*, in prose and verse; *Riddles*, in verse; *Jenny Wren*, a traditional extension to 'Cock Robin'; *Dick Whittington*, a near folk-tale; and an untitled booklet including 'The House That Jack Built'.

The nine upper titles all measure approx. 97×65 mm, and three of them (*We Are Seven, Jenny Wren, Birds and Riddles*) have sixteen pages, including the colour-washed covers. The other six all have thirty-two pages, with the outer leaves being pasted on to a cover of coloured paper.

'The House That Jack Built' appears in a smaller book (84×65mm) of twenty-four pages, including the paste-on cover. It is shown here in two copies: the coloured cover with moral verse by way of a title; the first page of the nursery rhyme, faced by alphabets.

the Opies' own circuitous journey to Westerfield House. In the *Cheerful Warbler* days they had been living frugally in Kensington, where their eldest son James was born, but the rigours of post-war London and a need for more space took them out of town in a south-westerly direction. They rented a cottage at Weybourne, near Farnham (next to 'The Elm Tree' public house), where work on the *Dictionary* – and acquisitions for the Collection – went forward steadily.

Thanks to Iona's mother-in-law, who gave practical help and looked after the children (a second son, Robert, was born – in a taxi-cab – in 1947, and a daughter, Letitia, in 1949), they were able to investigate the obscurities of their subject both in the British Museum library and in the Bodleian, where the papers of the antiquary Francis Douce proved to have fundamental importance. As the work proceeded, however, Iona and Peter Opie began to realize those truths which manifest themselves to all great collectors: that specialist knowledge gives you an advantage over everyone else and that any collection devoted to a specialized subject cannot help but grow outwards from its kernel.

Because of its revelatory status, *The Cheerful Warbler* may be seen to lie at the heart of the Opie Collection, but as progress continued with the *Dictionary*, it came to be joined by a rich hoard of companion works. At the same time, Iona and Peter Opie perceived that there were many interconnections between nursery rhymes and other kinds of children's book. To make sense of the nursery-rhyme collection, they argued, they should support it with a representation of other children's books from a given period, other books put out by nursery-rhyme publishers or illustrated by nursery-rhyme illustrators, other facets of children's reading – especially perhaps folk tales and poetry – to say nothing of a supporting library of reference books. Children's literature in its totality began to seem like the only justifiable aim for the Collection.

Rockbourne House at Alton, where the Opies lived 1949–59.

Weybourne Cottage could not long hold a hydra-headed monster of this kind and in 1949 the Opies moved ten miles, to Rockbourne House at Alton in Hampshire – which figures in the byline to the preface of the *Oxford Dictionary of Nursery Rhymes*, triumphantly published in 1951. By this time ambitions for the Opie Collection had moved beyond the printed word. Just as the *Dictionary* was to be followed by a sequence of equally authoritative works on the traditions of childhood – *The Lore and Language of Schoolchildren* (1959), *Children's Games in Street and Playground* (1969), and *The Singing Game* (1985) – so the books in the Collection were joined by the artefacts that mean so much to children in their own private world: toys, games, *trouvailles* – all those things from glass marbles to false noses that have potential to be loved recollections. What began life as a library of nursery rhymes was turning into a 'museum of child life'.

Rockbourne House was proving as little amenable to being turned into a museum as Weybourne Cottage was to being turned into a library, and during the last years of the 1950s house-hunting began again. Thus hove into sight the twin Noah's arks of Westerfield – which had lain unsold for seven years because they seemed so unmanageably cavernous – the very reason why they appealed to the museum-building Opies.[1] In 1959, therefore, the impedimenta

[1]The Opie archive preserves 676 sheets of estate agents' bulletins collected during the search that led to Westerfield.

of the great experiment were again packed up and travelled 'over the hills to West Liss', where, through more than twenty years, the Collection was to achieve world-wide recognition. The packing-cases (unopened) were of immediate use, since it was on them that the proofs of *The Lore and Language of Schoolchildren* were mostly corrected.

## WESTERFIELD

Perhaps the most vital characteristic of the Westerfield years (and in fair measure the years before) was the way in which the passionate adventure of collecting was harnessed to the dour disciplines of scholarship. The combination is not unique – as witness, in the Opies' own field, such investigative figures as James Orchard Halliwell, F. J. Harvey Darton and, in America, Dr d'Alté Welch – but the tendency is always rather for collectors to collect and to enjoy the pleasures of ownership and for scholars to explore: 'born to grapple with whole libraries', as Boswell's uncle said of Samuel Johnson.

There are good reasons for such division of labour – the best being that most collectors and most scholars see their activity as a full-time occupation which may only be intermittently intruded upon by other considerations. For

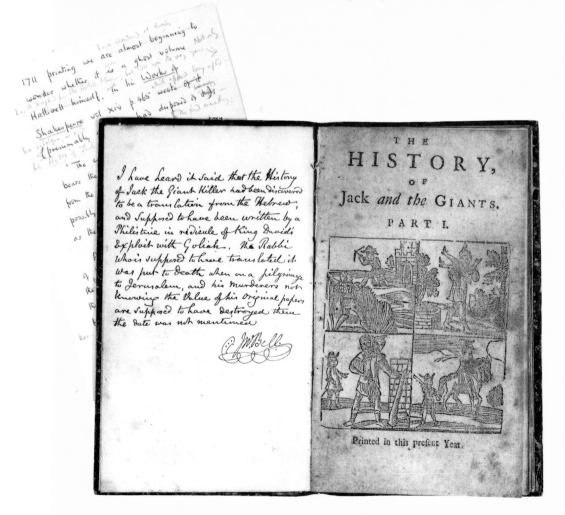

*The History of Jack and the Giants.* Part I. Printed in this present year (i.e. *c*.1740). 158×94 mm.

Peter Opie regarded this as the 'foundation text' for the printed versions of the classic English folk-tale. The picture shows manuscript notes in which he and Iona argue their way towards an explanation of the chapbook, obscurely published without date or place of publication.

the Opies, however – and especially Peter – there was a necessary and indissoluble link between the two. Collecting, for instance, might start the day. At breakfast-time catalogues would arrive, to be devoured alongside the cornflakes so that orders could be telephoned as soon as possible. If visits were made to libraries in London or Oxford, then time would be left for visiting shops to see what might have turned up – and not just bookshops or antique shops, either. Every collector will have stories of the unfindable jewel that turns up in a junk-shop – added to which are the barrows and the market stalls. Every Saturday morning, while Iona laid in groceries, Peter would raid the stalls in Petersfield market, and his Accession Diaries, where he recorded many of his purchases, bear regular witness to the rare or unusual things that he managed to acquire. By virtue of their reputation as specialists the Opies also gained the opportunity to buy many items privately before ever they were offered more widely; and by virtue simply of their virtue they were also given books or toys by owners who knew they would be 'going to a good home'. A copy of W. Oland Bourne's odd *Book of Fables Illustrated by Facts* (London: Nelson 1853) was sent to Peter in November 1963 from Hall's Bookshop, Tunbridge Wells: 'Please accept the enclosed with Mr Pratley's compliments'. A draft reply survives in Peter's handwriting:

> Mr and Mrs H. W. Pratley
> really oughter
> change their slogan
> 'Buyer, Seller and Exporter'
> to one more truly
> up-to-dater
> 'Buyer, Seller and Donator'

In his diaries Peter has stressed the consistent vigour with which the collecting of books, toys and ephemera was pursued. At the time, though, an increasingly sophisticated policy was followed of recording what had been acquired and assessing its comparative significance. In a series of files, notebooks and card-indexes, Iona and Peter Opie built up a huge body of information about their subject, cross-referenced to a degree that allowed relationships between items to be shown. Thus, in the case of their special interest in the eighteenth century (about whose children's books they contributed the section in the *Cambridge Bibliography of English Literature*), every book coming into the Collection would be not merely catalogued – any librarian could do that – but read and annotated, so that its place within its period could be assessed. Information about its acquisition might be recorded in Peter's Accession Diaries, and it might also be checked against a master-file of known books from the period located in other collections.

To be sure, the establishment of these interrelationships, which subsisted within the Collection and which also could be applied to the world outside, was largely possible because of the subject itself. If Iona and Peter Opie had found themselves undertaking research on fifteenth-century English printing, or Jacobean drama, it is hardly likely that they would have been able to build a powerhouse at Westerfield. But by investigating a neglected corner of popular culture, they were less dependent on any monopolies that might have been created by national or academic institutions. In a sense, they were forging their subject as they worked, and when they made discoveries they may have been the only people who were capable of recognizing them as such.

That was a hard-won privilege. The satisfaction of assembling so many 'treasures of childhood' was counterbalanced by the responsibility of knowing why these often derided or neglected things should actually be treasures and then by incorporating that knowledge into their work. Iona has given an account of the Westerfield routine which is chilling for those of us who are dilletantish enough to believe that simple things like toys and children's books are no subject for 'real' research:

'We made it a rule to be at our desks by nine . . . We knew we had to behave professionally; that a bohemian life-style would never result in our particular brand of book . . . We needed long hours of plodding and "fighting the damn words" (as Peter put it): our books were a welding of innumerable and sometimes intractable small elements into a reasoned and readable whole.

'Our method of working together was this. I sifted and analysed the folkloristic material that came in, entered it in the files, and sometimes wrote a summary of a particular game, while Peter did the same for children's book acquisitions. Each morning I took through to him the material for the next section of whatever book we were working on. He wrote the section and brought it back to me for written comment. This I returned to him for written counter-comment. Only after we had read all this writing did we discuss the piece verbally and sometimes we did not reach that stage until late at night . . .

'Looking back in the light of today's easier pace of living, our discipline seems almost superhuman. But we knew we had to write exceptional books that would go on selling and form a backlist, to produce royalties on which we could live. We knew that the two of us were the only work force we could command . . . and the only solution was to work long and regular hours. We had lunch at 1.00 p.m. and tea (a "workman's meat tea") at 6.00 p.m., then we went back to our desks for the profitable, uninterrupted evening hours . . .'[1]

Iona in her study at Westerfield House, with part of the reference library on folklore in the background.

[1] Slightly adapted from Iona Opie's article about herself in the 'Something About the Author Autobiography Series', Volume 6. Detroit, 1988, p.215.

*In Powder and Crinoline;*
*old fairy tales*, retold by Sir Arthur Quiller-Couch.
Illustrated by Kay Nielsen.
London: Hodder & Stoughton, n.d. [1913].

An illustration for the Grimms' story
of 'The Dancing Princesses' from one of the
'majestic colour-plate books'. Edwardian
elaboration here reaches a pinnacle of artificiality.
There is no correspondence between the
packed design and the plain tale.

Peter Opie taking down the box of 'Crazes 1930s'. This was early in 1964, just before the Temple was sliced horizontally to create the Archive Room above. The Temple (below), 'Peter's Room' and The Great Book Case (far left).

The picture we get here of double-headed, long-haul labour – two locomotives separate, but working together – requires a landscape to be constructed round it, the geography of those two Noah's arks. When Iona writes of herself 'sifting and analysing' the information on children's toys and games, we must see her in the front study at Westerfield, with two walls lined to the ceiling with books, 'the folklore collection' (which includes Lewis Carroll's own set of *Notes and Queries*: a periodical of incalculable value for Opie affairs); a third wall is shelved with the files in which the growing body of research on children's culture is organized.

Next door, a larger study, 'Peter's Room', was the heart of the children's book collection. It was dominated by a magnificent sextuple-fronted bookcase in which were housed many of the rarities (and, as time went by and as variant editions were added, the deep shelves came to be double-banked with little books). One long wall of the study – eventually named 'the Great Wall' – contained about fifteen hundred less important children's books, while other shelves, where the fireplace ought to be and in a huge island-bookcase, contained part of the reference collection. No fewer than three desks were also to be found, one of which was the centre for Peter's own extensive cataloguing and recording operations, and another of which acted more as a chest-of-drawers, containing rank upon rank of envelopes, in which were stored some of the most treasurable of all the 'treasures': over thirteen hundred little paper-covered chapbooks and popular books, and a wild miscellany of paper ephemera, including vulgar postcards and advertising gadgets, too entertaining to be allowed out of reach.

Beyond these two studies lay a scatter of rooms and passages whose walls and floor-space were gradually taken over in the service of the 'museum'. There was a farmhouse kitchen, lined with books on social history and education, with a huge run of *Punch* (attacked at one bad time by silver-fish); there was a tiled passage with boxed records of work done on the Opies' own books and with mountains of booksellers' and auctioneers' catalogues; there was the 'North Library' – so called in mock imitation of the British Museum's research reading-room – where half of the wall-space was given over to literature for adults and the other half, together with another island-bookcase, housed the fairy-tale collection, the natural history books and monstrous annual volumes of such periodicals as the *Boy's Own Paper*. Standing apart, august in a glass-fronted bookcase in the front hall, there was the nursery-rhyme collection.

Upstairs much rather random shelving had occurred to cope with part of the library extruded from the more comfortable quarters below: *St Nicholas* magazine sharing a passage-way with books on domestic affairs and, believe it or not, sport; school stories in one bedroom, majestic Edwardian colour-plate books in another. But two rooms and an attic were given over to some of the most splendid material in the whole house.

The first of these rooms, a fairly modest bedroom over Iona's study, was devoted entirely to more children's books. It came to be called 'the Knaster Room' after an old friend of the Opies', Roland Knaster, who had himself been a notable collector of children's books and whose collection was sold to the Opies to augment their own holdings.[1] At first sight, however, the Knaster Room looked more like part of a warehouse than a library. Admittedly it contained two handsome bookcases, but these had their glass fronts completely papered over, to protect the contents from sunlight, and the dominating feature of the room was a series of ceiling-high, slightly wobbly, steel racks which contained some nine hundred uniform-sized cardboard boxes. Within these boxes, all carefully labelled and cross-referenced, were a sequence of books by authors from Aesop to Wyss, another sequence on subjects from Alphabets to The Zoo, and many groups which did not fit into any clear alphabetical scheme: books from foreign parts, books that approximated in one way or another to toys, and a host of painting, tracing and drawing books. The fact that everything was hidden away in boxes and not displayed regally on shelves should not have deluded visitors into thinking that the Knaster Room was a repository for less significant parts of the Collection, not worthy of public exhibition. Many of those cartons contained books or manuscripts or drawings of exceptional rarity – acknowledged in some instances by velvet linings applied to the cardboard interiors.

Next door to the Knaster Room came the Temple – so called not for any

[1]Roland Marcus Ignatious Knaster really deserves a separate memoir all to himself. All that can be said here is that his collection, largely assembled between the two World Wars, contained some remarkable European children's books and some pristine examples of English children's books from the 1920s and 1930s, almost all of which were additions to rather than duplications of Mr and Mrs Opie's books.

One of the boxes from the Knaster Room open to show an upper compartment lined with red velvet and arranged to display four books published by John Marshall, all bound in varied patterns of Dutch flowered paper (that is a decorative paper, probably originating in Germany, embossed with a floral design and then coloured with dabs of paint and dusted with gilt):

*The Entertaining History of Little Goody Goosecap*, n.d. [c.1788]. 117×78 mm.

*The Adventures of a Pincushion*, Vol. I by Mary Ann Kilner, Marshall's Infants Repository, n.d. [c.1782]. 116×75 mm.

*Tales and Fables* selected by T. Ticklepitcher, printed and sold by John Marshall, printers and booksellers to the Good Children of Great Britain and Ireland, n.d. [inscr. 1785]. 117×76 mm.

*The History of England in Verse*, n.d. [c.1787]. 104×66 mm.

reasons that had to do with the worshipping of rare pieces but in recollection of 'Fuller's Temple of Fancy', one of those little commercial emporia set up by the print and paper-toy sellers during the late eighteenth and early nineteenth centuries. At the start of things the Temple was just a large billiards room, but soon after moving into Westerfield the Opies undertook major surgery on the place. The room was sliced in half horizontally, creating an Archive Room above, just tall enough for Peter Opie to stand in upright (other people had to stoop). Thus the room retained its ludic character. Daylight was blocked out of the windows, and glass cases for display were bought for £10 the lot from the Commonwealth Institute, who were moving their premises.

In this way a room was constructed which could at once house many of the artefacts of childhood and also provide space for displaying pieces or groups of particular interest. Another multitude of cardboard boxes lined the east wall, opposite where the window ought to have been, and these contained such mouth-watering delights as kaleidoscopes and yo-yo's, and such mystery objects as Jacob's ladders and rubber-bulb toys. The huge illuminated glass cases on the north wall contained a 'permanent exhibition' of particularly significant (and perhaps unboxable) artefacts, such as sections of model railways, while the central, horizontal display case could be used either for book exhibitions or for showing toys and games. Underneath it there were drawers, as in a plan-chest, which contained a wonderful miscellany of paper samples, writing-sheets and posters. The stairs on the south wall led up to yet more stores in the Archive Room, where were kept many miscellaneous antiquities such as christening clothes, conjuring sets and Boy Scout ephemera.

From this bald description of the piling up of good things at Westerfield the impression may well be given that the Opie Collection was a miscellany on the verge of turning into a muddle. On the contrary, the Collection was carefully shaped and controlled to illustrate not just what children enjoyed but how

*Cinderella; or, the little glass slipper.* Versified and beautifully illustrated with figures. London: printed for S. & J. Fuller, 1814. 132×100 mm.

One of the productions of the 'Temple of Fancy'. Peter Opie regarded the Fuller series of 'doll-dressing' books as being of historic importance for the way in which they compounded characteristics of toys, picture books and graphic inventiveness in a single artefact. The Opie Collection thus has a fine run of these items which are all too often found lacking the cut-out heads, or the hats, or other garments.

adults intervened in the child's life, quelling enjoyment with catechisms, or harnessing enjoyment in the fond hope that it might have an educational effect, or pandering to enjoyment with base commercial vigour. Meanwhile an overriding awareness of the way the fashions of society impinged on society's children gave coherence to the assembled evidence – which formed a kind of gigantic jigsaw puzzle, parts of which were more or less filled in and parts of which consisted of isolated pieces.

In retrospect the making of the Collection appears a quixotically ambitious undertaking for two reclusive scholars. For while it is true that they had opportunities no longer open to incunabulists and the like, they were nonetheless working on a subject which had suffered from other depredations as severe as those caused merely by the passage of time. On the one hand there was the hopeless failure of children to realize that their picture-books, or their teddy bears, or their spinning-tops were objects that later generations would come to venerate. Mutilation and destruction abounded. On the other hand there was a similar failure on the part of adults to see anything of consequence in childish toys. 'Lusisti satis', says the (now Olympian) narrator in *The Golden Age,* 'enough of play', and the objects of childhood are sacrificed to the dustman, the salvage collector and the bonfire.

Under these circumstances it is not surprising that collectors must take what they can when it appears and hope that, by good fortune, they may fill out and supplement elements of their collection as time goes by. For the Opies – beginning simply with books – there was a ready-made commercial tradition within which they could work, securing through the interconnecting services of 'the trade' the opportunity to form a collection that would come close to displaying every aspect of the history of children's literature in some depth. The subject may not have figured very prominently on the horizon of booksellers, auctioneers, librarians or bibliographers when Peter seized upon *The Cheerful Warbler,* but at least a framework of communication was present through which collecting could be pursued. (And, of course, as the Opies pursued it, and as their publications and their influence mounted up, so they formed part of a strongly running tide which elevated both the status and the prices of children's books as collectible objects. On several occasions in his later diary entries Peter both rejoices in his good fortune at having anticipated this upswing in interest and laments the growing impossibility of affording books which were becoming the quarry for rich institutions and millionaire collectors in places a long way from Hampshire.)

Compared to the system within which book-collectors went about their business, the market for the toys and ephemera of childhood was altogether more amorphous. This meant that a different policy prevailed in developing that part of the Opie Collection that lay beyond the printed word. Instead of aiming for an impossible totality (impossible to achieve and impossible to house, even in Westerfield), they developed the idea of 'representation'. The Opies' knowledge of children and children's natural proclivities allowed them easily to map out the huge variety of 'things' that play a part in the child's recreative life, and the aim of the Collection moved towards representing examples of these 'things' in whatever evolutionary stages might be

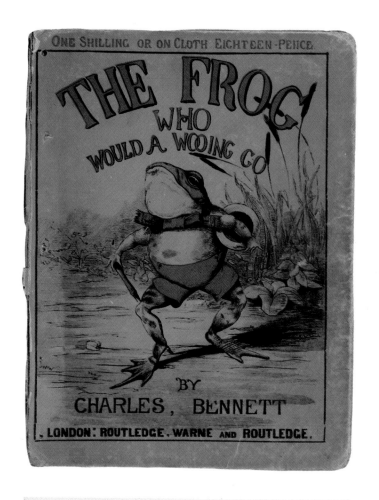

*The Frog who Would A-Wooing go.* By Charles Bennett. London: Routledge, Warne & Routledge, n.d. [*c.*1860]. 212×165 mm.

The complete pictorial record of the frog's luckless expedition as made into a picture book by Charles Bennett. The peculiar layout, with two narrow pictures to a page, comes about because Charles Bennett had originally planned the book to be half its final page area.

"Pray, Mr. Frog, will you give us a song?
Let the subject be something that's not very long."

"Indeed, Mrs. Mouse," replied the Frog,
"A cold has made me as hoarse as a hog."

"Since you have caught cold, Mr. Frog," Mousey said,
"I'll sing you a song that I have just made."

As they were in glee and merrymaking,
A Cat and her kittens came tumbling in.

The Cat she seized the Rat by the crown,
The kittens they pulled the little Mouse down.

This put Mr. Frog in a terrible fright,
He took up his hat, and he wished them good night.

As Froggy was crossing it over a brook,
A lilywhite Duck came and gobbled him up.

So here is an end of one, two, three—
The Rat, the Mouse, and little Froggy.

attainable. The ambition always existed to collect, where possible, the first manifestation of a toy or game and to show something of its later history – and if, in some cases, there developed an opportunity to possess a large range of variant manifestations (like glass marbles), then so much the better. Iona and Peter Opie shunned the dilletantism implicit in putting together a mere 'cabinet of curiosities', but the putative Opie Museum of Childhood was to be an informed collection of *exempla* rather than a comprehensive centre for research.

## DISPLAYING THE COLLECTION

The division that subsists between books and 'toys' in the Opie Collection makes for some difficulty in deciding how best to display its treasures in the confines of a single book. For although Iona and Peter Opie conceived of the Collection as an homogeneous unit, to be called upon in many different ways to support their explorations of the world of childhood, there can be no argument that the book part of the Collection formed a resource of formidable stature, whereas the toys made up a richly varied, but by no means so definitive, complement.

In one sense this represents a curious imbalance. For after all, if we consider the various artefacts that surround fortunate children as they grow up, we do not see them overwhelmed with books to the exclusion of everything else. The child's book – whether a rag-book, when their chief use for the thing is to chew it, or a picture-book, when they look rather than read, or a close-printed adventure story, when they creep down under the blankets with a torch after lights-out – takes its place within a personal pantheon along with teddy bears or fivestones or electric train-sets. So it may seem perverse to be devoting a substantial part of a book on 'the treasures of childhood' to books alone, but it is inevitable, for two main reasons.

The first is that (*pace* teddy-lovers and model-railway enthusiasts) children's books are amazingly diverse within their fairly standard format. No doubt it is dangerous to say, 'if you have seen one Dutch doll you have seen the lot' – but that is certainly not so dangerous as saying the same thing of picture-books or adventure stories, where the personalities of authors and illustrators will lead to almost absolute differences between one book and the book next door.

The second reason concerns the sheer longevity of books as adjuncts in a child's life. Not only are children's books far more diverse than many simple toys but, in England, they have a history of over three hundred years, within which there have built up long chains of influence and evolution. Every generation (or every second or third generation) will find itself confronted by a range of books very different from those of its predecessors, and yet that range will have grown out of the earlier ones and will in its turn affect the nature of the later ones. 'Children's books' turn into a wood whose trees have to be looked at very carefully.

For these reasons (which to some extent governed the formation of the Opie Collection) – and for the further plain reason that the Opie Collection of

Children's Literature is one of international stature – the book section of this survey of the total collection of child life at Westerfield will be devoted to describing some of the bibliographic treasures, and endeavouring to explain why they should be seen as such. The second half of the survey will seek to show something of the tumultuous assembly of toys and games and to demonstrate their varying significance in the world of childhood.

The illustrations for our display have been chosen as far as possible to stress both rarities in the Collection and objects which have served the humane purpose of giving children pleasure. Here too, though, a (defensive) stress has to be laid on the intractability of books as subjects for illustration. For while the reader may find it quite easy to take in the nature of glass marbles from a picture of glass marbles, he cannot take in a whole book simply by looking at a picture of the title-page (although in some cases the publishers made a big effort to help him to do just that). The stories are to be read from end to end, the pictures are to be gloated over one after another; thus, of necessity, we can only occasionally give an extended view of objects that are more dynamic than they seem.

*Gordon Craig's Book of Penny Toys.* Published at the Sign of the Rose, Hackbridge, Surrey. 1899. 316×253 mm. [No. 17 of a putative 550 hand-coloured copies]

A book to symbolize the Opie ideals, for not only is it an imaginative book for children about toys, but it is also a work of some rarity. Rumour has it that Edward Gordon Craig destroyed a quantity of his stock to save himself the labour of colouring the pictures. This is hinted at in the Opie copy, which contains a letter from Craig to E. W. Thomson of Brighton saying: 'it takes some time to bring the book out as all the pictures are coloured by hand'.

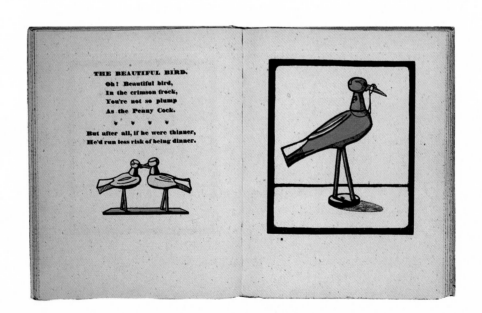

# PART ONE

# THE BOOK
# COLLECTION

# WHAT MAKES A TREASURE?

The peculiar *frisson* experienced by the collector of children's books is not as easy to explain as you might think. Frequently enough it is put down to mere nostalgia – finding again that cheap edition of *The Fifth Form at St Dominic's* that was the solace of a suburban childhood; or escapism – opting out of the difficult business of living for something more schematic and controllable; or despair – shoring up the ruins of lost illusions with fragments of *The Beano*. But such accounts are as erroneous as they are predictable.

As we have already seen, the Opie Collection had its inception in curiosity rather than nostalgia (and curiosity tends to be a central motivation for many bibliomaniacs). A desire to investigate a subject – or a single book within that subject – is joined by a desire to own the needed resources, and as the Collection progresses so the territory expands within which curiosity may grow. When Peter bought *The Cheerful Warbler* in 1945 almost nothing was known about the minutiae of 'Children's Literature' as a field for the collector (and indeed not much more is known today). The result was that with book after book – often apparently of the most insignificant kind – features of special interest yielded themselves up, revealing the unusual if not the absolutely rare.

This combination of the unusual and the rare is what gives character to the Opie Collection, and the quest for ever more intriguing examples brought a continuous tremor of excitement to the Opie household. To begin with there might be the discovery through a catalogue or through hearsay that a desirable book was on the market and then there would follow the *mauvais quart d'heure* – or often longer – when fortune hung in the balance, when it was not certain if the book would or would not be acquired for the Collection. Peter's diaries contain regular accounts of the tribulations of the book-hunter – jumping on trains to catch up with a rumoured rarity, waiting impatiently for replies to letters or answers on the telephone.

One of these diary entries gives a particularly keen insight into the sway of emotion that is almost inescapable for collectors with the ambitious designs of the Opies. On 12 July 1974 Peter records how, almost casually, he had come across a copy of James Janeway's *A Token for Children Part Two* (1672) in a general catalogue put out by George's, the booksellers in Bristol, who described it as 'very rare' and priced it at £30. They were right in their description, for only one other copy of the book is known (in the Osborne Collection at Toronto Public Library), but perhaps they were tentative in their price, for this is among the earliest of all English children's books designed for 'recreational reading' – even though its sequence of anecdotes about small children dying in a state of grace may not suggest such a thing. In any event, the arrival of a copy on the market – if only of Part Two – had been enough to interrupt Peter's comfortable breakfast on the morning of Tuesday, 9 July:

'I looked at the postmark and saw, with resignation, that it had been posted on the 6th – Saturday. It was already a day old. But I went to the phone, although it was not yet nine, and stuck on the phone, letting the bell go on ringing (fortunately Bristol is now on STD) until a quarter past nine, when it was answered by – one of my worse fears – someone who said the catalogue department was engaged, but that he would give them a message. By past experience I know this means (a) that the person or persons responsible for the catalogue have not yet arrived, and (b) that when the person or persons do arrive, they start taking orders, and only learn of my order after what I wanted has been promised to someone else. My feelings, after this phone call, plunging and tossing between hope and despair, the hope that I might be becoming the possessor of one of [the] rarest and most desirable of children's books – for a sum (unlike at Sotheby's) that I could easily afford – and the fear that I might miss it by human error or tardiness or disinterestedness, were too awful for me now to look back upon. The more so as the man at the other end did say that orders for the catalogue had "started coming in" only that morning. I even rang again, half an hour later, on the pretext of ordering another book; and had the same reply as for the first call, which almost made the situation worse.'

After all this high-tension anguish the *Token* did finally arrive at Westerfield, but, on being unpacked, turned out to be 'a drab little book', not quite measuring up to its undoubted status as a treasure, and – Peter wryly noted – it now seemed 'of no special consequence to possess it'. Such a down-beat, not to say blasé, remark may have been occasioned in part by a natural reaction to the torments of placing the order to begin with (and in part by the

*A Token for Children*, The Second Part. By James Janeway. London: printed for Dorman Newman, 1672. 115×63 mm.

The text lives up to the lugubrious prospects held out by the title-page, here reproduced in full. Nevertheless, Janeway's intention was to exert persuasion by giving children stories that he thought they might like to read, and, in doing that, he was helping to establish a new tradition of addressing the child reader through narrative.

His success was not short-lived. His book continued in print through half the nineteenth century, as witness this title-page from a near-chapbook edition:

*Janeway's Token for Children*, London: T.C. Johns, 1836. 108×68 mm.

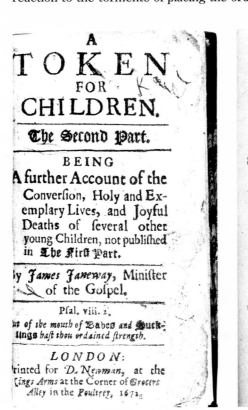

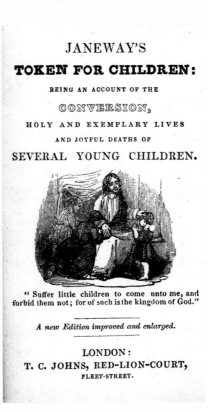

fact that, when that diary-entry was being written, Mr and Mrs Opie were entertaining glamorous media-people who were interviewing them for *The World this Weekend*).

Nevertheless, making allowance for such distractions, the comment still seems slightly surprising, coming as it does from a collector who appreciated better than anyone the gap that exists between drab appearance and historical vibrancy. Most readers of this present volume, for instance, might well have not looked twice at Janeway's *Token* if it had turned up in a tenpenny jumble sale; and most readers may well be puzzled over the excitement occasioned by a little book with no claim to either literary or physical distinction (to say nothing of possible surprise over its monetary value: for if the *Token* were to come up for auction today it would probably fetch at least fifty times the price assigned to it in George's catalogue). But Peter Opie rarely lost his intense feeling for the circumstances of a book's 'presence' – what it had to tell of the lives of those who wrote and published it and of the children who read it – and, in so far as one of the glories of the Opie Collection is the depth of its holdings of material from the formative years of children's literature, so it requires a certain sympathetic awareness, a certain imaginative effort, to perceive how significant these rarities may be.

The scarcity of a book in numerical terms is not the only factor that makes for rarity, however. The drabness of the *Token* may well militate against a wide appreciation of its importance, but the presence of many books in the Collection that are anything but drab (in appearance, anyway) offers the chance of a more immediate response. The indignities to which children's books are subjected by their young readers have already been mentioned, and are known to most of us, so the treasurable nature of copies that turn up unpawed by jammy fingers or with no signs of use as a flail is fairly easy to comprehend.

A distinction can be drawn, however, between two aspects of the visual appeal of children's books. On the one hand, the appeal of finding a mint copy is simply the wonderment at its mere survival. Thus when we contemplate some of the brilliant examples of eighteenth-century children's books in the Opie Collection – still firm, as though they had never been opened, glowing in their gilt bindings, or even refulgent with hand-coloured illustrations – or when we look at some of the pristine annuals and picture-books from Victorian times, we gain a privileged sense of seeing these books as their first purchasers would have seen them.

At a more 'aesthetic' level on the other hand, there is the fact that children's books have played an important role in the development of graphic design – which may include the arts of typography, of illustration, of book-binding – and the preservation of important examples of this development is itself a contribution to the history of the book arts or the history of an artist's career. Thus, at one end of the time-scale, there are the decorative designs for bindings which Thomas Bewick made during his brief spell in London and, at the other, the illustrations by Jan Lewitt and George Him for Juljan Tuwim's *Lokomotywa* (Warsaw, 1938), brought to England – along with the illustrators themselves – in 1939 and inspiring new ideas about the making of picture-books (see pages 32 and 41).

*FRONTISPIECE*

*Tales of Passed Times by Mother Goose. With morals.* Seventh ed. corrected and adorned with fine cuts. London: printed for T. Boosey, 1796 [preceded by a title-page in French]. 172×102 mm.

Although this is not an original illustration by the American engraver, Alexander Anderson (he was copying a French original), the copper-plates are an example of his reproductive skills. They are said to have been shipped to England to make this London edition of Perrault's tales.

Another readily recognized characteristic that confers particular glamour on a book – though not necessarily for children – is its historical significance as 'the first' of its kind. Indeed, the antiquity of Janeway's *Token* contained an element of 'firstness' about it, but the notion is much more broadly applicable than that. Thus it is easy to understand why Peter Opie should have been so enthusiastic about obtaining, say, his first edition of Thomas Hughes's *Tom Brown's Schooldays* (1857) – not just because it is a famous book, difficult to find in its original state (as the Opie copy), but because it is a book that stands at the start of, and deeply influences, a long-running fashion in fiction for children. Other examples might be the collection of Perrault's *Tales of Passed Times*, published in London by T. Boosey in 1796, but illustrated with plates engraved by the American craftsman Alexander Anderson: probably the first example of the importation of American talent to embellish children's books; and the 'New Scenic' *Little Red Riding Hood*, published by Dean & Son round about 1863. This may not be the first 'movable book' – which is not just a book with moving parts, but it could also be said to be a book that is 'moving' in the direction of becoming a toy – for it stands very near to the beginning of the commercialization of 'movables' during the Victorian period.

All these kinds of treasure are examples of books which fall into general categories – scarce books, fine books, first editions, and so on – but the Opie Collection is also notable for its holding of what Peter liked to call 'individual copies'. These need not be a distinctive part of any particular category: rather they are books which take on significance by virtue of their own, individual history.

Without doubt the most famous 'individual copy' in the Opie Collection is that of *The Wind in the Willows* inscribed by Kenneth Grahame for his son Alistair, to whom the adventure of Toad was first told as a bedtime story. But although there is nothing of the same air of romance about it, the copy of *The Fairy Spectator* by 'Mrs Teachwell', inscribed 'Love attends dear Edward Frere From His Affec^te Friend The Fairy', has a recherché attractiveness, for after all, Mrs Teachwell is known to be Ellenor Fenn (née Frere) so that this would seem to be a presentation copy to her – perhaps – nephew (who has dutifully filled in two names obscured by dashes in the Dedication: 'Miss M[ills]' and 'E[llenor] F[enn]').

In a different vein there are books that carry other kinds of association, for instance *A Visit to the Bazaar*, an account, with pretty hand-coloured engravings, of various tradespeople, published by John Harris in 1818, but bearing in the Opie copy the book-plate that Kate Greenaway designed for her patron Frederick Locker-Lampson; or the dimly insignificant 'reading easy' that was owned by the youthful Algernon Charles Swinburne; or the dozens of books that were owned by lesser mortals who nonetheless wrote in them, or drew in them, or converted them from pious books to lottery devices – thus leaving behind a token of the interplay between readers and the printed word.

Of all such 'individual copies', however, none are quite so individual as those highlights that are the holograph manuscripts and drawings, though there are relatively few of these. Of the manuscripts the most important is a transcription by William Roscoe of his famous set of verses 'The Butterfly's

The bookplate (84×68 mm) which Kate Greenaway designed for her friend and patron Frederick Locker. He was a keen collector of children's books and this plate appears in his copy of *A Visit to the Bazaar*. London: for J. Harris, 1818.

*The Wind in the Willows*. By Kenneth Grahame. New York: Charles Scribner's Sons, 1908. 188×125 mm.

Kenneth Grahame's inscription in the copy of his famous story that he gave to his son Alistair, for whom the central tale of the adventures of Toad was told. No one has been able to explain why Grahame should have given him the American edition. Possibly, as a fastidious bookman, he thought it more elegant.

Ball', subject of over a dozen picture-books in the Collection; and of the artwork the finest appears in the set of line-proofs for Randolph Caldecott's *Hey Diddle Diddle* and *The Milkmaid*, coloured up by the artist as a guide for his printer. Much of the rest of the holograph material is more mundane,[1] but it includes a remarkable eighteenth-century harlequinade (see page 53) together with some experimental jokes, all of which work on the principle of folding paper flaps, and also a variety of MS books which range from a carefully made copy of the picture-book version of Goldsmith's *Mistress Mary Blaize* after the edition by John Harris, to a mixture of unpublished works. Some of these, like a group of preliminary drafts for various modern pop-up drawings, were clearly intended to be published; others, like *The Autobiography of a Doll; a physio-cum-psychodollological narrative* (dated 1879), were clearly produced for personal satisfaction or family entertainment.

But if such a miscellany of manuscripts does not finally amount to a holding that reveals much about the trade in children's books, at least it confirms the Opie Collection's role in giving insight into the complex relationship between children, adults and the written or printed word. The modest informalities betokened by books copied, or books invented for a particular child, or books written and illustrated by children themselves, can be as illuminating or as touching as the manuscripts of the published literature itself.

'The Butterfly's Ball'. Ms. 247×195 mm.

This manuscript copy of one of the first carefree poems written for children is in the hand of its author, William Roscoe, who appears to have inscribed it for his son Thomas. The text differs from the early published versions and is probably a revision, or an imperfectly recollected transcription.

[1] Except for the unexpected *Comic Alphabet Illustrated* by Amelia Frances Howard-Gibbon. This pictorial version of the nursery poem 'A Was an Archer' is already known about because a manuscript exists in the Osborne Collection at Toronto, which has been published through the good offices of the Friends of the Osborne Collection. Mr and Mrs Opie, however, possessed what appears to be a superior copy by the same artist, apparently the original, which had been submitted for a prize. In the Opie copy the first picture is fully coloured.

Her love was sought I do aver,
By twenty Beaux and more:
The King himself has follow'd her,——

——When she has walk'd before.

*Dr Goldsmith's Celebrated Elegy on that*
*Glory of her Sex Mrs Mary Blaize.* Published Nov. 1. 1808 by
L. Harris [sic.]. Ms. 135×110 mm.

A manuscript copy of the picture-book published by
John Harris in 1808. Both the
copying and the amateur binding have been done with great
panache, and their degree of
accuracy is of less import than the conjectural reasons for
why the task was undertaken.
Was it done purely for pleasure; or as an exercise; or to give
to someone; or to be kept by someone
who could not afford the 1s. 6d. for a coloured copy?

Right: *The Polite Academy;*
*or school of behaviour for*
*young gentlemen and ladies.*
Fourth ed. London: printed
for R. Baldwin, n.d. [*c*.1778].
116×72 mm.

Bound in paper over boards.
The two engraved pictures
on the front and back covers
are almost certainly work
which Thomas Bewick did
during his brief sojourn in
London in 1777.

Below: *The Minor's Pocket*
*Book for the Year 1791.*
London: printed for the
proprietors and sold by Wm.
Darton & Co., n.d. [1790].
129×70 mm.

Title-page and folding
frontispiece of a rarity that
drew from Peter Opie some
of his most uninhibited
exultations. This book-cum-
diary was published from
about 1790 onwards and
became famous as the work
that gave Ann and Jane
Taylor (the authors of
'Twinkle, twinkle, little star')
their entrée into publishing.
Little can be told of it,
however, because practically
no copies have survived from
the thirty years or so during
which it was published. The
father of the children's book
historian F. J. Harvey Darton
(a relation of the original
seller of the *Pocket Book*)
sought a copy for more than
twenty years early in this
century (offering as much as
£50 for one) and met with no
success.

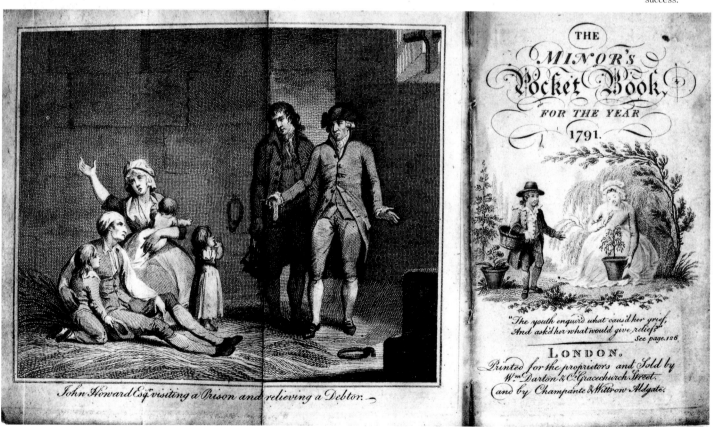

*The Barn That Tom Built. A new game of forfeits.*
Embellished with sixteen coloured
engravings. London: printed and sold by John Marshall,
1817. 164×108 mm.

An adaptation of 'The House That Jack Built', probably
illustrated by Robert Cruikshank
and here seen in its original cover of glazed paper with a
printed and hand-coloured label.
The colouring both outside and inside the book is as bright as
on the day it was done.

*The Flight of the Old Woman
who was Tossed up in a
Basket.* Sketched and etched
by Aliquis. London: published
by D. Bogue, 1844
204×105 mm.

Panoramas preceded pop-ups
(see page 61); few have ever
been as ambitious as this
example, made to open out
vertically, and measuring
more than seven feet when
fully extended. The unknown
'Aliquis' also etched a five-
foot-long *Pictorial Humpty
Dumpty* (1843) which
included translations of the
rhyme into four languages.

How Humpty Dumpty the Kings Favorite sat upon a wall.  How the same Humpty Dumpty fell off the wall.  How the King having heard of his

to the spot and superintended in person the raising of the prostrate

ites    misfortune    ordered    out    all    his    horses    and    all    his    men    repaired

mpty    How the king's attempt to raise his favorite failed.    How the weight of Humpty Dumpty was so

reat that he dragged forward many of the King's men, and how the rope breaking, all the rest for many miles fell backwards.

The long and changeable schooldays of Tom Brown. Peter Opie accounted his purchase of the first edition of *Tom Brown's Schooldays* (Cambridge, 1857) as one of the triumphs of the Collection, for it is a scarce book at the best of times and especially so in the fine original state of this copy, with its blue, ripple-grain cloth binding still sound.

From its first appearance the book achieved wide popularity and established the school story as a distinctive genre in English children's literature. This selection from many editions in the Collection shows some of the styles in which the book appeared, and shows too how often the book reached its readers as a wholesome present or as a school prize:

By an Old Boy [i.e. Thomas Hughes]. Cambridge: Macmillan & Co., 1857. Unillustrated. The first edition.

With a preface by Lord Kilbracken, and introduction, notes and illustrations, edited by F. Sidgwick. London: Sidgwick & Jackson, 1913.

Illustrated by Harold Copping. London & Glasgow, Collins Clear Type Press, n.d. Inscribed 'John Pearse. For an improvement in Pianoforte Playing & for splendid work in Theory and Music from E. Stocker 1913.'

London, Ward, Lock & Co. Ltd, n.d. Illustrated with black and white plates by H. M. Brock. A prize label reads: 'Wesleyan Sunday School, Wesley St., Ossett.

Presented to Arthur H. Jowett for regular attendance and good conduct, 1905.'

London, Macmillan & Co., 1904. Illustrated with black and white plates by J. Macfarlane. The pictorial binding carries an LCC prize stamp in gold, and there is a prize label: 'London County Council. Aristotle Road School. Awarded to Wm. Cann for excellent conduct and attendance and praiseworthy attention to his work during the year 1906. J. G. Ball Head Teacher.'

Left: *Little Red Riding Hood.*
London: Dean & Son, n.d.
[?1863]. 248×172 mm.

A primitive pop-up book,
operated not (as today) by
the leverage of the book's
hinges, but manually. The
reader pulls a ribbon behind a
flat picture and it pops up to
an angle of 90°.

From the publisher's
number-code on the cover it
would seem that an edition of
12,000 copies of the book
was prepared in 1863. Few
workable copies now remain.

*Peeps into Fairy Land.*
Edited by F. E. Weatherly,
London, Ernest Nister. n.d.
[*c.*1895].

A colour lithograph three-
dimensional scene bringing a
hint of romantic theatre to an
otherwise commonplace
story-book. Although Nister
printed in his native
Germany, most of his
authors and artists were
British.

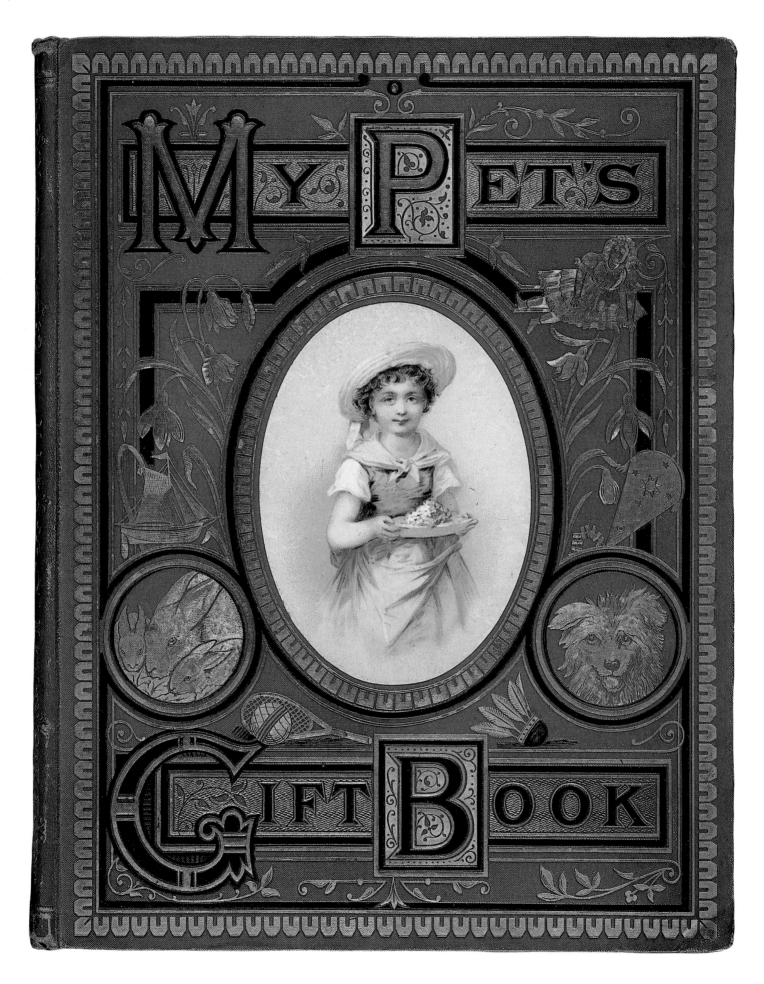

*Locomotive*. By [Juljan] Tuwim, illustrated by [Jan] Lewitt and [George] Him. London: Minerva Press, 1939. 180×250 mm.

During the 1930s influences from Continental Europe began to affect British book design and illustration. Here, on the brink of the Second World War, is a now scarce translation from Poland whose bold illustration using offset lithography was to influence much subsequent work. (As 'Lewitt-Him' the artists went on to illustrate the first of Diana Ross's 'Little Red Engine' books, and their style was reflected in Leslie Wood's pictures for later books in the series.)

*My Pet's Gift Book*. London: The Religious Tract Society, n.d. [1878]. Cover: 250×190 mm.

Although Victorian cloth bindings make a tougher covering for a book than glazed paper wrappers, they have been equally vulnerable to violent usage. Crisp examples like this, with the coloured paper onlays still unmarked, are not easy to discover.

# THE BEGINNINGS

ow far any kind of literary history is precisely defined in most people's consciousness is matter for doubt. Nevertheless, it is arguable that a certain 'period flavour' attaches itself to the names of such writers as Chaucer and Shakespeare and Samuel Johnson, bringing with it an awareness of difference, if not of evolution.

Where children's literature is concerned, little of such general awareness – however vague – exists. Few people have much notion of when children's books began to be a serious part of commerce, and very little historical differentiation is made between one well-known children's book and another. This may well be caused in part by the far shorter time-span within which children's literature has developed as against literature for adults. In addition the general concept of 'children's literature' is dominated by a few classic books rather than by Chaucerian, Shakespearian or Johnsonian authors who epitomize an age. The classic books turn up alongside each other in standard series: *Grimms' Fairy Tales* and *Alice*, *Little Women* and *Kidnapped*; and they merge together as a vaguely defined 'heritage' rather than as distinct manifestations of different attitudes about children's books, stemming from distinct times and places.

For this reason insufficient justice will be done to the Opie Collection of Children's Literature if it is merely described through examples, as in the last section, isolated to show what may distinguish a 'treasure' from the general run of children's books. At cost of being repetitious, it is necessary to emphasize Peter Opie's ambition to make the Collection a complete survey of the history of children's literature in all its development, and, as in any collection, the more run-of-the-mill exhibits give clearer definition to the highlights.

Although it may seem overweening to think in terms of a 'complete survey', Iona and Peter Opie very nearly achieved this in their collecting of children's books for the eighteenth and the first decades of the nineteenth century. At one time Peter noted that 'all eighteenth-century children's books were represented' in the Collection in one edition or another, and although that is not strictly true it does give force to a view that the early books in the Opie Collection form a kind of corporate treasure, aside from the many outstanding 'individual copies'.

As we have already seen with Janeway's *Token*, the Collection does contain some remarkable examples from the period from the mid-seventeenth century onwards, when 'children's literature' (of a sort) was beginning to emerge – and although one may have some doubts about the eligibility of the *Guide for the Child and Youth* (1723) for this category, Peter Opie certainly rejoiced in its acquisition as one of his great triumphs. But so hazy was the concept of a 'children's book' in this early period, and so few copies of so few titles have survived, that most collectors, even in the 1940s, would think themselves lucky to assemble any sort of cross-section of what is known.

From about 1740 onwards, however, the momentum of children's book publishing changes dramatically. The key figures in this change are two London publishers, Thomas Boreman, 'near the Two Giants in Guild-hall', and Mary Cooper, 'at the Globe' in Paternoster Row, who did two things that had not been done before. First they demonstrated practically – and not simply by lip-service – that there was a place for playfulness in children's books, and second they incorporated this idea into making what today we would call a 'children's list', a group of books consistently edited for the market of the times. Boreman did this primarily through his now famous 'Gigantick Histories' (1740–3) which were, in fact, miniature books, mostly about the sights of London, but which also treated the child-reader as a human being rather than as a receptacle for information. Mary Cooper – who was an extremely active bookseller – was less consistent in her approach, but through books like *The Child's New Play-thing* (1742) she introduced a new light-heartedness into the business of learning to read. (She was also responsible for publishing arguably the greatest treasure in the whole of English children's literature: *Tommy Thumb's Pretty Song-Book* of *c.*1744, the first published collection of nursery rhymes – not, alas, in the Opie Collection, for it is known only by a unique copy of its second volume in the British Library.)

Neither Thomas Boreman nor Mary Cooper made a dominant place for themselves as children's book publishers at this time. The first died early, probably in 1743, and the second seems to have had too many fingers in too many pies to develop her interest in children's books as a speciality. What they probably did do, however, was to work as an inspiration on the man who really did put children's books on the commercial map: John Newbery, bookseller, of the Bible and Sun in St Paul's Churchyard. Newbery perceived the potential of the ideas in Boreman's and Cooper's publications and over nearly thirty years he developed the making and selling of children's books into something which is recognizably 'modern'.

Iona and Peter were rightly proud of their holdings of Newbery books (which should be taken to include not just the books published by John Newbery up to his death in 1767, but also later reprints and additions to the list put out after his death by, on the one hand, his son Francis and his manager Thomas Carnan, and on the other, quite separately, his nephew Francis and, later, his nephew's widow Elizabeth[1]). What these holdings confirm, however, is the vigour of Newbery's commercial activity rather than his commitment to a completely enlightened programme of children's entertainment. Many of the books may have seemed over-didactic or dull even to their earliest readers, but they were designed and marketed (to use two modern expressions) in a way that sought to convince otherwise.

One of the most treasurable Newberys in the Opie Collection, the second edition of *The History of Little Goody Two-Shoes* (1766), is a case in point. The story is ham-fisted and ludicrous, but the book achieved near-classic status because of its engaging title, because of the way that this lent itself to advertising, and because of the book's attractive get-up – not least 'the cuts by Michael Angelo'. Everything that Newbery did had the bounce and energy

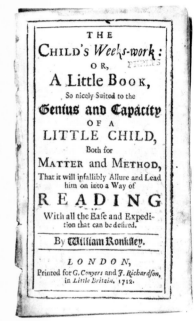

*The Child's Weeks-work.* By William Ronksley. London: printed for G. Conyers and J. Richardson, 1712. 130×80 mm.

An unillustrated book soberly printed throughout. But, as may be gauged from this title-page, it was one of those revolutionary works that tried to teach reading through entertainment. With its attractive and remarkably undidactic range of simple poems and fables, it ought to have been successful.

that had earned him the nickname 'Jack Whirler' from Samuel Johnson, and the Opie Collection holds testimony to his innovative powers. We see the range of his publishing, from primitive picture books like *A Pretty Book of Pictures* (14th ed., 1787 to 'Tom Telescope's' weighty *Newtonian System of Philosophy* (4th ed., 1770); we see him making an abortive effort to start the first periodical for children, the *Lilliputian Magazine* (2 copies: *c.*1752 and 1772); and we see his constant interest in the illustration and binding of his books. He took over from earlier publishers like Boreman the idea of binding books in 'Dutch flowered paper' and made great play with the result in such advertising phrases as 'prettily bound and gilt'.

The other reason for assigning importance to John Newbery is simply that he was successful, and success in the book trade almost automatically leads to the compliment of imitation. If one publisher can make money out of the new genre 'children's books' then others will try, and straight away channels open for an expansion of the market and for a degree of experimentation that will seek to develop different angles of approach.

The Opie Collection affords great scope for charting the progress of this expansion, which is still not recognized for the wide movement that it was. Among early books, for instance, that perhaps owe as much to Mary Cooper as to John Newbery, there could be mentioned the *Little Polite Tales, Fables & Riddles in Easy Verse* published in London by R. Baldwin, junior, in 1749, or the second edition of the *Little Master's Miscellany* that was printed in Birmingham by T. Warren, a figure who is only just beginning to emerge from the shadows as an active maker of children's books. Also prominent among the products in those velvet-lined boxes in the Knaster Room were the little books of the publisher John Marshall, who became very active as both printer and publisher in the decades after John Newbery's death, often by battening on to Newbery's ideas. The Collection contains well over a hundred Marshall publications (including his take-off of *Goody Two-Shoes* in *The Renowned History of Primrose Prettyface*, *c.*1782), and when these are placed alongside the books of at least twenty other London publishers and at least thirty provincial ones who were working during the latter part of the eighteenth century, we begin to see how the Collection serves to improve our understanding of the period's attitude to its offspring.

*A Collection of Entertaining Stories.* Vol. II. Worcester: printed for S. Gamidge, n.d. [c.1785]. 112×75 mm.

A remarkable survival from the little-known premises of a Worcester bookseller (although Vol. I seems to have disappeared for good). The 'entertaining stories' include the 'History of Little Jack Horner' and 'Little Red Riding Hood', and Gamidge proudly advertised his wares on the front end-paper, pasted down on the book's pretty Dutch paper cover.

*The Lilliputian Magazine.*
London: printed for the
Society and published by T.
Carnan at Mr Newbery's,
n.d. [?1752]. 112×65 mm.

Probably the first periodical
ever published for children,
but only known, as here, with
the parts reorganized to
make a book (slightly akin to
a twentieth-century
Christmas annual).
  Records of the issue of
individual parts survive in the
printer's ledgers. The
'Society' was made up of
subscribers to the magazine,
and is here used by Newbery
as a publicity gimmick.

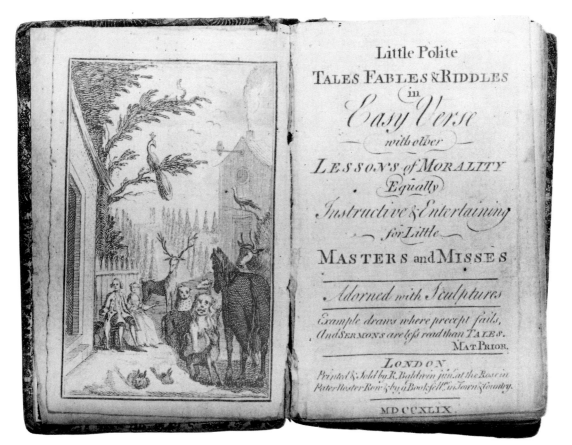

*Little Polite Tales, Fables &
Riddles in Easy Verse.*
London: printed and sold by
R. Baldwin jun., 1749.
95×62 mm.

A very rare book of fables
and 'other puerile
amusements', adapted to the
new ideas for making
children's books more
approachable. Title-page and
frontispiece, shown here,
were printed in red.

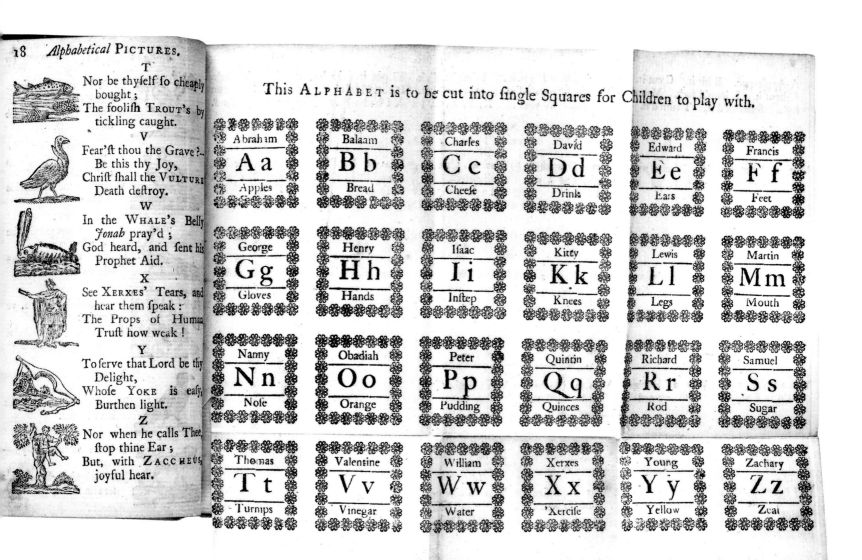

18 *Alphabetical* PICTURES.

**T**
Nor be thyself so cheaply bought;
The foolish TROUT's by tickling caught.

**V**
Fear'st thou the Grave?..
Be this thy Joy,
Christ shall the VULTURE Death destroy.

**W**
In the WHALE's Belly *Jonah* pray'd;
God heard, and sent his Prophet Aid.

**X**
See XERXES' Tears, and hear them speak:
The Props of Human Truft how weak!

**Y**
To serve that Lord be thy Delight,
Whose YOKE is easy, Burthen light.

**Z**
Nor when he calls Thee, stop thine Ear;
But, with ZACCHEUS joyful hear.

This ALPHABET is to be cut into single Squares for Children to play with.

| | | | | | |
|---|---|---|---|---|---|
| Abraham **Aa** Apples | Balaam **Bb** Bread | Charles **Cc** Cheese | David **Dd** Drink | Edward **Ee** Ears | Francis **Ff** Feet |
| George **Gg** Gloves | Henry **Hh** Hands | Isaac **Ii** Instep | Kitty **Kk** Knees | Lewis **Ll** Legs | Martin **Mm** Mouth |
| Nanny **Nn** Nose | Obadiah **Oo** Orange | Peter **Pp** Pudding | Quintin **Qq** Quinces | Richard **Rr** Rod | Samuel **Ss** Sugar |
| Thomas **Tt** Turnips | Valentine **Vv** Vinegar | William **Ww** Water | Xerxes **Xx** 'Xercise | Young **Yy** Yellow | Zachary **Zz** Zeal |

*The Child's New Play-Thing*: being a spelling-book intended to make the learning to read a diversion instead of a task. Eighth ed. London: for Messrs Ware, Hawes, Clark, etc., 1763. 150×80 mm.

First published by Mary Cooper in 1742, this is one of the books that brought a new liberalism to children's reading. Not only does it introduce the alphabet game on a fold-out, shown here, but it also includes illustrated alphabet verses, fables and traditional stories like 'St George and the Dragon' and 'Reynard the Fox'. Four editions in the Opie Collection, from the second of 1743 to the ninth of 1775, attest its popularity.

*A Choice Collection of Hymns and Moral Songs* by several authors. Newcastle: printed by and for T. Saint, 1781. 125×72 mm.

A greatly enlarged wood engraving by the young Thomas Bewick for the 'moral song' on the whipping of tops ('Obstinate tempers will nothing perform . . . etc.'). The book is one of many similar little semi-didactic works published by T. Saint, often with pictures by Thomas or John Bewick. All are very rare.

MORAL SONGS.

SONG XXI.

*On the whipping of Tops.*

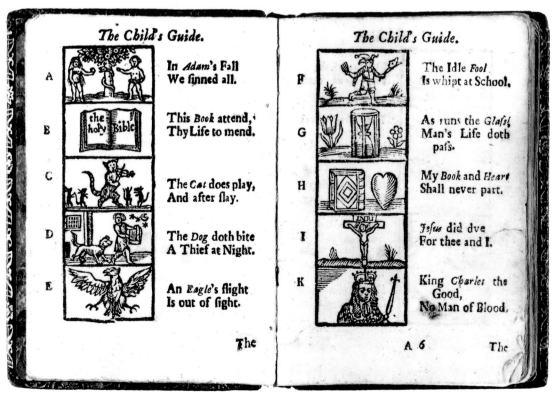

*A Guide for the Child and Youth.* By T. H. *M.A.* London: printed by J. Roberts for the Company of Stationers, 1723. 94×69 mm.

Two sectioned woodcuts illustrating the first ten letters of a pictorial alphabet. The couplets are of much earlier date than 1723 (as may be guessed by the reference to King Charles) and they are notable for their appearance also in the first book for children printed in America: the *New England Primer.* Here they are among the cheerful aspects of a work which combines religious and secular lessons.

*The History of Little Goody Two-Shoes.* A new edition, corrected. London: sold by J. Newbery at the Bible and Sun, 1766. 94×57 mm.

Only one copy is known of the first edition (1765) of this celebrated work (in the British Library), and only two copies seem to have survived of the second, revised edition shown here.

Below: *Westminster Abbey.* Vol 1. By the author of the Gigantick Histories. London: printed for Tho. Boreman, bookseller, 1742. 60×44 mm.

Enlarged reproduction of a page-opening of this miniature description of the sights of the Abbey, the first of three volumes. The pleasant, unassuming text gains character through such things as the 'gigantick' joke, and a charming prefatory 'Ode on the Vanity of Ambition'.

*Little Goody Two-Shoe*

# THE
# HISTORY
OF
Little GOODY TWO-SHOES;
Otherwise called,
Mrs. MARGERY TWO-SHOES.
WITH
The Means by which she acquired her Learning and Wisdom, and in consequence thereof her Estate; set forth at large for the Benefit of those,

Who from a State of Rags and Care,
And having Shoes but half a Pair;
Their Fortune and their Fame would fix,
And gallop in a Coach and Six.

See the Original Manuscript in the *Vatican* at *Rome*, and the Cuts by *Michael Angelo.*
Illustrated with the Comments of our great modern Critics:

A New EDITION, Corrected.
LONDON:
Printed for J. NEWBERY, at the *Bible* and *Sun* in St. *Paul's Church-yard,* 1766.
[Price Six-Pence.]

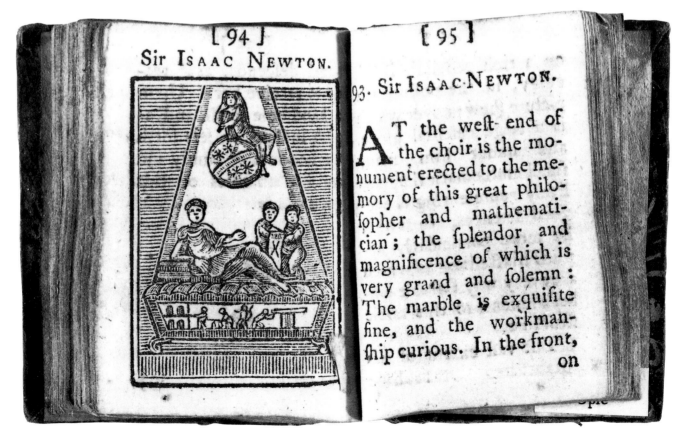

( viii )
### The STUDENT.

F ROM a Wretch cloath'd with Rags, begging
    Alms at a Gate,
To a Nobleman bleſs'd with a plenteous Eſtate;
I am rais'd by my Learning, my Virtue and Truth,
And may this be the Fortune of every good Youth.
                     The

( 1 )
### The LION and JACKALL.

W HILE the bold Lion beats the Wood
    His faithful Jackall finds him Food;
And then at Diſtance ſtands aſide,
Nor eats till firſt his Lord's ſupply'd.
                  B

*A Pretty Book of Pictures for Little Masters and Misses.*
Fourteenth ed. London: for T. Carnan, 1787.
100×85 mm.

A simple book containing verses and descriptions about
birds and beasts. As the title implies, though, the
selling-point lay in the woodcuts that appeared frequently
throughout.

# NURSERY NOVELTIES

o matter how much competition in children's books was engendered during the eighteenth century there was not a great deal of variation in the general format and appearance of what was produced. The limited size and capacity of the presses on which the books were printed, the need to control costs in what was clearly a cut-throat business, ensured that most of the children's books of the time were of a fairly uniform modesty of design.

One exception was the arrival during the 1760s of the fashion for 'harlequinades' or 'turn-up' books. These are entertainments that work on the flap principle. You print your text, with accompanying pictures on two same-size sheets of paper, one laid on top of the other and secured along top and bottom edges. The top sheet is then divided into panels which can be turned up to reveal appropriate (or inappropriate) continuations of the text and pictures on the sheet below. Modern versions often make play with the creation of monstrous forms by the interchange of heads, bodies and legs. Strictly speaking, the eighteenth-century turn-ups were adjuncts of the theatrical industry, rather than the children's book trade, but they have their origins in an example from a hundred years earlier, clearly intended for the young, and there is no doubt that children enjoyed them (and, indeed, harlequinades were later published only for children).

As has been noted above, one of the treasures among the Opie Collection of manuscripts is a six-panel turn-up, made for a child by his aunt in 1741 and following closely the seventeenth-century foundation text *The Beginning, Progress and End of Man* (1650), which was created with primarily didactic

*Mother Shipton, or Harlequin in the Dumps.* London: Robert Sayer, 1771. 182×75 mm.

No. 9 in Sayer's series of 'turn-ups' which ran to more than a dozen numbers, most of which are now hard to find. This is a hand-coloured copy, sold for a shilling, as against 6*d.* plain.

intentions. The Opie Collection also contains several examples of the harlequinades that were manufactured for general distribution, mostly by Robert Sayer, and mostly employing texts of an extraordinary banality that did not do justice to the possibilities of the 'turn-up' idea.

Nevertheless, turn-ups are important for more reasons than their existence as primitive forerunners of pop-up books. In the first place they were examples of a growing use of metal-engraving and a growing fashion in printing whole products on the engraver's press (rather than on the standard upright letterpress machine). By printing an entire sheet, both text and pictures, from a single engraved plate, some useful economies in production costs could be made, and although the process was not suitable for large-scale works, and although the plates tended to wear very quickly, these were not necessarily disadvantages for the publisher of short and ephemeral works like children's books.

The second great stimulus that was provided by harlequinades was also, broadly, a technical one: the introduction of colour. For although the engraved sheets of the turn-ups were printed in black and could be sold thus (the Opie Collection has a couple of monochrome examples from the publisher John Roberts[1]), it is more usual to find them with hand-colouring done before publication and they were advertised as '6$^D$ Plain 1$^S$ Colour'd'. The result is attractive and eye-catching and there is no great surprise in discovering the practice shifting across to conventional books too. The London publishers, Tringham, who went in for harlequinades in the 1780s, were among the first to issue children's books that could be sold either plain or hand-coloured.

The technical changes – or the widening potential of new production methods – foreshadowed in the harlequinade industry were to reach a sudden, dramatic fruition in the publishing events that occurred at the beginning of the new century. Almost overnight the makers of children's books seem to have realized that they did not have to preserve a standard approach to their job, current since the days of John Newbery, and a whole series of innovations followed one another hot on each other's heels.

The energetic John Marshall was in the forefront of this revolution, in league with that Fairy Spectator encountered above, 'Mrs Teachwell'. Between them they had been devising new methods of teaching children to read and to count, through the use of apparatus like cut-out letters, picture-cards and counting-beans sold in boxes that were a bit like 'home-teaching' kits. John Marshall (probably with Mrs T.'s assistance) further developed the idea by creating a special library for the young child sold in its own box, which was made and decorated to look like a bookcase.

This *Juvenile, or Child's Library*, with its eighteen paper-bound volumes and its drawer to hold a 'portfolio', is the subject of one of Peter Opie's most amusing book-hunting anecdotes. Apparently, in April 1968, he had seen the *Library* advertised in the *Bookmarket*, going for £30 from a music shop in Wisbech. But on telephoning them he found that the item had just been sold to Derek Gibbons, a bookseller at that time in Norwich. After an exchange of postcards Peter arranged to visit Mr Gibbons in order, at the very least, to make notes on the *Library* for the forthcoming *New Cambridge Bibliography of*

[1] The titles are: *The Comical Tricks of Jack the Piper* and *Dr Last; or the devil upon two sticks*. This latter is of special interest, partly because it is the upper sheet only of the harlequinade, fully printed, but not yet divided, and partly because it exactly corresponds to a second *Dr Last* in the Opie Collection, published by Sayer. In other words there are signs here of either collaboration or piracy.

*English Literature.* 'The very least' was operative because Derek Gibbons was eager to sell the box for dollars rather than pounds – but after they had talked for eight hours (!) Peter triumphantly notes: 'In the end I got it.' (Among the more influential factors in the negotiations was Mr Gibbons' liking for the idea that the *Library* would be part of the Opie Collection.)

The arrival of *The Juvenile, or Child's Library* was not to be an isolated success in the representation of John Marshall's inventive influence at the beginning of the nineteenth century. For alongside this 'large' library Iona and Peter Opie were eventually able to place its best known stable-companion, *The Infant's Library* (sixteen tiny books in a 'library box' – but in rather poor state), and the only known set of a rival publisher, Fairburn's *Cabinet of Instruction and Amusement* (1802).

Nor did Marshall stop at books in boxes. Through the establishment of some production unit, perhaps slightly akin to the workshops in Colombia that produce today's pop-ups, he undertook a busy trade in picture-making that went in various directions (he even attempted a *Pictorial Magazine*). One manifestation was the production of sets of educational cards on various themes, packed into their own specially labelled 'cabinets' and accompanied by prettily bound miniature books that gave (necessarily brief) descriptions of the contents.

Much of this zestful new activity owed its inception to the ease with which publishers were accustoming themselves to using a combination of engraved work with hand-colouring. Plant and resources were clearly available and they were nowhere more energetically exploited than in the making of children's picture-books – a decidedly simpler operation than that of constructing miniature libraries.

The eighteenth century had not quite formulated the idea of a picture-book. Certainly publishers had put out plenty of works that conform to the rough definition of being books where text and pictures work together as roughly equal partners. Excluding the untypical harlequinades, there were alphabet-books and fable-books and rhyme-books and scatalogical riddle-books which made great play with illustrations, but these never seem to have been seen by their makers in more than accidental terms. They were not a genre open to exploitation.

That changed rapidly from 1800 onwards. At that time publishers with their own engraving shops, like William Darton, or with close links to engravers, like the puzzle and games firm E. Wallis, began to make greater use of engraved plates for both cards and books – sometimes using plates for the whole book in the way that the harlequinade merchants had done for their goods. The idea was seen to have possibilities, and on 1 June 1805 the publisher John Harris produced the book that was to crank up the presses as they had never been cranked before. This was *The Comic Adventures of Old Mother Hubbard and her Dog* – a version, or perhaps an expansion, of a traditional ditty, written by a young lady called Sarah Catherine Martin – issued by Harris in an edition which had text and uncoloured illustrations printed together from copper engravings and was neatly bound in plain tinted paper.

A Manuscript Harlequinade. 1741.

This home-made 'turn-up', drawn in pen-and-ink, with touches of pink and blue, is hinged with thread and stitched into marbled paper covers. The panels follow their seventeenth-century model fairly closely, showing: (1) Adam, (2) Adam, Eve and Serpent, (3) Cain, (4) a Lion turning into a Griffin, (5) a Heart [lacking back panel], and (6) Man and Death. The inscription reads, rather erratically: 'William Wood his Book Gin Him by his Eant Franke Mariot 1741.'

The Serpent being the Subtilst Beast,
Of any in the Field
Full soon had he beguiled Eve
And made her for to yield.
She did not regard the Great loss
But tasted of the forbidden Tree.
And wo'd you see the further Cross
Turn up the Leaf and you may see.

The little book was an instant success, which may be judged first by the fact that, by 1807, it had reached a twenty-fourth edition, and second by its immediate consequences. Harris, who realized that he was on to a good thing, at once cashed in on it by publishing a few months later a *Continuation* by Sarah Catherine Martin, a *Sequel* 'by another hand', and an extension of the method to other parts of pet-land with *Dame Trot and her Cat* and its *Continuation* (all 1806).[1] Not to be outdone, other publishers pitched into the new fashion and before long the bookshops would seem to have been awash with small square children's books, got up in the style of *Old Mother Hubbard* but questing after alternative forms of jollification and nonsense. (As it happened, John Harris was again to hit the jackpot in 1807 when he made a little engraved book out of William Roscoe's children's poem 'The Butterfly's Ball' [see above, p. 30]. This too had an instantaneous success and was responsible for sparking off dozens of imitations, of which some in the Opie Collection are: *The Peacock 'At Home'* and *The Lion's Masquerade* by Mrs Dorset, *The Elephant's Ball* by 'W. B.', *The Horse's Levee*, *The Butterfly's Birthday*, *The Lobster's Voyage to the Brazils*, and – most affectingly – *The Butterfly's Funeral*.)

The representation of early picture-books such as these in the Opie Collection is one of its glories. They formed part of the large quantity of ephemera housed in the desk drawers in 'Peter's Room', and they offer perhaps the most immediate insight into the pleasure that collectors of children's books get from their quaint pastime. For these books do not work their spell merely by being scarce – and by being especially scarce in clean, bright condition; they also work it by being part of the first large-scale publishing movement in children's literature that set out uninhibitedly to supply entertainment.

Iona and Peter Opie have already used their Collection to show something of the inventive energy of that movement by reprinting twenty-seven of these picture-books in *The Nursery Companion* of 1980. The large page size of that anthology does not give a completely satisfactory replication of the homeliness of these little books, and its lithographic printing cannot bring back the delicacy of their hand-colouring, but the texts have been well chosen to reveal how hospitable a modest sixteen pages could be to alphabet rhymes and nursery verses, traditional stories and contemporary satire, offering a type of comical instruction that could deal with anything from 'punctuation personified' to a simple guide to musical notation.

The period is also interesting for its experiments with kinds of book outside the normal sixteen-page format, such as Darton's battledores and Tabart's attempt at a story panorama. There is a piquancy too in seeing the publishing venture presided over by serious-minded William Godwin attempting to adapt the copperplate formula to social commentary, and a pleasure in seeing the involvement of George Cruikshank and, more especially, his brother Robert, in some of the more frolicsome entertainments. Children's books were perhaps beginning to attract more than casual notice from writers and artists who were past their apprentice years and more than mere hacks.

CHARITY

GAFFER GRAY
Printed for The.* Hodgkins, Hanway Street, May 26. 1806.

*Gaffer Gray: or, the misfortunes of poverty, a Chistmas ditty.* London: published at the Juvenile Library, 1808 [cover title]. 120×90 mm.

Said to be written by Thomas Holcroft, the radical, *Gaffer Gray* was published by his comrade-in-arms, William Godwin, at his precariously financed bookshop in Skinner Street.

Social polemic is thus introduced into the 'Mother Hubbard' format. Gaffer Gray gets no help from Parson Trulliber, Lawyer Doublefee or Squire Guzzle, and must needs be entertained by a comrade almost as poor as himself.

*The Juvenile, or Child's Library.* A wooden box, with a sliding lid, fashioned to look like the front of a bookcase. Behind the lid are four compartments and a drawer, containing (mostly improving) little books and a 'portfolio' which probably once contained a map. The whole outfit was 'published' by John Marshall in 1799 and was one of the period's most prominent portents of a new spirit of diversity and playfulness in the making of books for children.

The box measures 280×185×82 mm and the books within are of two sizes: 115×76 mm and 95×76 mm.

[1] Just as our knowledge of the Newbery publications has been enhanced by S. Roscoe's bibliography, so we owe a detailed account of John Harris to another scholar (working without academic support, for the challenge – and love – of the thing): Marjorie Moon, *John Harris's Books for Youth 1801–1843; a check-list.* Revised edition Winchester, St Paul's Bibliographies, 1986.

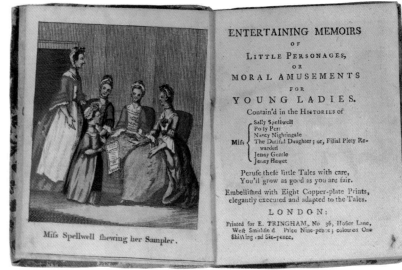

Miss Spellwell shewing her Sampler.

ENTERTAINING MEMOIRS
OF
LITTLE PERSONAGES,
OR
MORAL AMUSEMENTS
FOR
YOUNG LADIES.
Contain'd in the HISTORIES of

Miss {
Sally Spellwell
Polly Pert
Nancy Nightingale
The Dutiful Daughter; or, Filial Piety Re-
warded
Jenny Gentle
Jenny Hewet
}

Peruse these little Tales with care,
You'll grow as good as you are fair.

Embellished with Eight Copper-plate Prints,
elegantly executed and adapted to the Tales.

LONDON:

Printed for E. TRINGHAM, No 36, Hosier Lane,
West Smithfield. Price Nine-pence; coloured One
Shilling and Six-pence.

*Left: The Infant's Cabinet of Trades.* London: John Marshall, 1802.

Here Marshall is seen trying a different ploy: a wooden box containing twenty-eight engraved picture cards, coloured by hand. Two miniature books accompany the set to give the child reader an explanation of the pictures. Marshall issued boxes of this kind on some ten subjects and this is the only complete set known of the 'Trades' series. The box measures 92×63×39 mm, the cards 73×48 mm, and the books 48×38 mm.

She went to the Hosier's
To buy him some hose,
When she came back
He was drest in his Cloaths.

Above: *Entertaining Memoirs of Little Personages.* London: printed for E. Tringham, n.d. [?1788]. 107×85 mm.

On the title-page is the legend: 'Price Nine-pence; coloured One Shilling and Six-pence'. That evidence, coupled with the consistency of the colouring throughout this copy, makes it almost certain that this is an example of publisher's colouring, and not embellishment by a youthful owner. Copies of trade-coloured books as early and as fine as this are extremely rare.

Left: *The Comic Adventures of Old Mother Hubbard and her Dog.* [By Sarah Catherine Martin] London: J. Harris, 1805. 116×95 mm.

As well as inventing at least some of these verses about Old Mother Hubbard, Miss Martin sketched out some accompanying pictures which were converted to engravings when the text was published. The Opie copy of this famous book appears to be the only extant copy of the second printing (and only one or two copies have survived of the first).

*London Cries.* [12 cards wrapped in white paper with an engraved, hand-coloured label] [London] Sold by Williams & Thomas Darton, n.d. [*c.*1808]. 51×91 mm.

The cries with their traditional images given in alphabetical sequence.

*Morals for Children.* [12 cards in a blue paper wrapping with a printed, hand-coloured label] London: W. Darton & J. Harvey, 1799. 93×70 mm.

These prettily designed and coloured cards were clearly forerunners of (and an influence on?) Marshall's experiments. They treat solemn moral issues, whether as fables or as direct admonitory verses, and stand in contrast to the other series from the same publishing family shown opposite:

*Richardson's New Battledore.* Derby: Thomas Richardson,
n.d. [?1830]. 142×93 mm.

Battledores were folded cards, usually with rudimentary
lessons printed on them: alphabets,
numbers, catechisms. (Their name presumably derived
from their alternative, informal use as
playthings.) In this late example a cheerier editorial
policy has prevailed and the alphabet
has been converted into a set of pictorial puzzles
based on games and activities.

*R. Cruikshank's Comic Alphabet.* London: Darton & Clark, n.d. [c.1840] [cover title]. 178×108 mm.

The comedy lies chiefly in the phrases which Robert Cruikshank has chosen to illustrate or in his punning interpretations. His brother George had also published a *Comic Alphabet* in panorama form in 1836.

*A True History of a Little Old Woman, who Found a Silver Penny.* London: printed for Tabart and Co., 1806. 132×105 mm.

This traditional story, otherwise known as 'The Old Woman and her Pig', is illustrated in this book, incident by incident, with hand-coloured engravings. The cumulation of events then unreels itself in the final, four-panel panorama shown here – a most ingenious idea for its time.

The Opie Collection has three copies of this scarce book. All are different. The copy illustrated here is probably of the first edition, which appears to have been printed in a hurry since in later printings the engraving is more refined.

# MOTHER BUNCH, MOTHER GOOSE AND MOTHER HUBBARD

I n all the foregoing survey of how a developing children's literature is exemplified in the Opie Collection only glancing references have been made to those forms of traditional discourse – folk-rhymes and folk-tales – which prompted the Collection in the first place.

This is in large measure because traditional literature led a very obscure existence during the foundation of the children's book market. From earliest times education had looked askance at the 'bawdy ballads' or the 'feigned fantasies' that we all recognize as having an immediate appeal to untutored youth, and in a climate where 'the trade' needed to assure the public of the probity of its wares it was not inclined to make too much play with the attractions of works which might be suspect in the eyes of 'the parents, guardians and nurses in Great-Britain and Ireland' (Newbery's phrase).

Nevertheless, throughout the eighteenth century uncoordinated forays were being made into the store of traditional literature. Publishers of some repute could be found providing versions of fantasy-tales which were resonant with possibilities. They may have concealed 'folk' elements in a fairly dignified dress, but they brought into currency a fund of narrative that could be reworked and resold through the penny-book trade and thus find a popular audience for itself. The haphazard nature of much of this publishing – and the scarcity of evidence – makes for difficulties in estimating its effect on either adult or child readers. What can be said, though, is that only through the relentless source-hunting of scholars like Iona and Peter Opie can we begin to draw firmer conclusions about the reception of folk literature in this period of drought.

The Opie Collection has some remarkable examples of the early publication of traditional tales in England (apart, that is, from the universally appreciated, but altogether more sophisticated, romances). Much of the material hailed initially from France, and the Collection boasts among its earliest treasures the first two volumes of the first English translation (from the French) of the *Arabian Nights Entertainments*, dated 1706.[1]

From the same early period the Collection also has both French and English editions of fairy tales by Madame D'Aulnoy, whose unpronounceable name was eventually acclimatized as 'Mother Bunch'. She was a very ornate editor, building round what may have been a traditional core to her tales a complex web of incident and psychological characterization, but, without much local competition, her stories were apparently welcomed in England, and tales like 'The White Cat' and 'The Yellow Dwarf' may be counted among the most popular of the century. (See pages 72-73.)

Without doubt her sobriquet of 'Mother Bunch' was invented to chime with, or imitate, that now more widely respected fairy-tale dame, Mother Goose,

*The Famous and Renowned History of Sir Bevis of Southampton*. Printed for W. Thackeray, 1689. 187×135 mm.

Not a children's book, but a good example of a popular story published for a readership that would have included children.

[1]Only one other pair is known with this date – at the University of Princeton. Peter Opie's acquisition of this set from the catalogue of a Cornish bookseller was achieved over the head of the Bodleian Library, who did not get to the telephone quickly enough. The bookseller reported that the Library was slightly miffed since it thought Mr Opie was straying from his territory of 'children's books'.

whose first appearance was also in France, with the publication of the *Histoires ou Contes du Temps Passé*, 'edited', so it is assumed, by Charles Perrault but said to be by 'Ma Mère l'Oie'. This little collection, which is incontestably the most famous in the world, was first published in Paris in 1697, at about the same time that Madame D'Aulnoy's stories were first appearing, but instead of her intricate fantasies 'Ma Mère l'Oie' set down plain tales in the manner of a nursery storyteller and established in 150 pages or so the classic forms of such narrations as 'Cinderella' and 'Blue Beard', 'Sleeping Beauty' and 'Puss in Boots', 'Hop o' my Thumb' and 'Little Red Riding Hood'.

From the point of view of today's comparatively enlightened publishing trade there seems to be no good reason why Perrault's *Contes* should not have immediately leapt into the world bestseller lists. They had all the attributes needed for economic success – brevity, simplicity, popular appeal – and yet for some decades they seem to have been overshadowed by the more elaborate tales of the courtly writers, and in England the first translation appeared only in 1729, more than twenty years after various editions of Madame D'Aulnoy. And even when it did come out it does not seem to have taken the market by storm. The *Histories, or Tales of Past Times*, alternatively named in the frontispiece as 'Mother Goose's Tales', made only sporadic appearances throughout the century, sometimes being published more as an English/French reading-book than as a book of nursery entertainment.

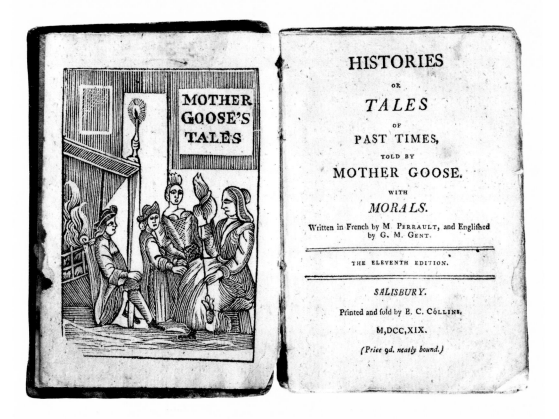

*Histories or Tales of Past Times*, told by Mother Goose. With Morals. Written in French by M. Perrault, and Englished by G. M. Gent. The eleventh edition. Salisbury: printed and sold by B. C. Collins, 1719 [i.e. 1799]. 112×78 mm.

Perrault's world-renowned tales in an edition typical of those published for children in the eighteenth century, and one in which Elizabeth Newbery was also involved. This is the copy that (unbelievably) misled several commentators into positing a much earlier appearance for the book in England than the generally accepted 1729. The other 'Newbery' Perrault in the collection is dated 1777.

As always, though, we are hampered in assessing the full impact of the book by the dearth of recorded copies. In that context the eighteenth-century Perraults owned by the Opies are a distinguished tribe, with several examples of texts in English and French combined, and with two out of only three known copies of the various Newbery editions listed in S. Roscoe's bibliography.

Evidence for the popularity of 'Mother Goose's Tales' does not depend solely on known editions however. Just as important is the extent to which individual tales were taken up by the makers of nursery books and chapbooks on the look-out for marketable texts. Just as fables and truncated romances found their way into Mary Cooper's innovative *Child's New Play-thing*, so other 'home-reading books' like the *Pretty Book for Children* brought in tales from Mother Goose. But the incidence is not high and the widespread adoption of French tales as grist for the mills of picture-book production was another feature of the publishing fashions revolution that took place at the beginning of the nineteenth century.

Indeed, that pattern of sporadic, uncoordinated activity, followed by wholesale exploitation, is almost exactly matched by the popular genre that was indubitably for children: the genre of nursery rhymes. As the first focus of the Opie Collection, and as the element most completely sustained through the forty years of the Collection's growth, nursery rhymes can almost be seen as a model for what happened to the publication of children's books in general. Their treatment shows in miniature the shifts in taste and in publishing fashion that affected all books for children as the trade developed from the mid-eighteenth century onwards. What is more, the actual collecting of them also offers a model for the interaction of book-hunting and scholarship – for as Peter Opie himself said, one of the traditions of Mother Goose literature is that it tends to be extremely scarce.

Perhaps the first thing to note about the Nursery Rhyme Collection is that, chronologically, its foundations don't appear to have much to do with the subject at all.[1] They are made up of unexpected works like *Queen Anna's New World of Words*, an English-Italian dictionary first published in 1598, wherein are quoted the last two lines of:

> To market, to market,
> To buy a plum bun:
> Home again, home again,
> Market is done.

There is a manuscript commonplace book of about 1665, in which someone has written the rigmarole 'I saw a peacock with a flaming tail', and there is a collection of proverbs, printed at Cambridge in 1670, which includes the earliest known version of 'Jack Sprat'. Such disparate books as these precede any attempt by publishers to make up collections of nursery rhymes, and they help to provide slim evidence for the currency of the rhymes as an accepted part of daily life.

When rhymes do appear in publications for children – with Mary Cooper's

( 65 )

Youth, fooner or later, be rewarded, who taketh Pains to read, and find out the Meaning thereof.

*The* Story *of the* Little Red Riding-Hood.

ONCE upon a Time there liv'd in a certain Village, a little Country Girl, the prettieft Creature ever was feen. Her Mother was excelfively fond of her; and her Grandmother doated on her much more. This good Woman got made for her a little Red Riding-Hood, which became the Girl fo extremely well, that every Body call'd her *Little Red Riding-Hood.*

F 3                              One

*A Pretty Book for Children; or an easy guide to the English tongue.* Vol. I. London: printed for J. Newbery and for B. Collins in Salisbury, 1758. 100×70 mm.

'Little Red Riding Hood' is here incorporated into a book 'perfectly well adapted' to 'the tender capacities' of children in the first stages of their education. The Vol. II that followed was a more resolutely factual *Museum for Young Gentlemen and Ladies.*

The Opie copy of *A Pretty Book* is apparently the only known copy of the eighth edition and came to light only after S. Roscoe had finished his wide-ranging Newbery bibliography.

[1]Most of the facts and comments in this section necessarily depend heavily on Iona and Peter Opie themselves. For not only have they, in the *Dictionary* of 1951, set out a canon for the English nursery rhyme, with discussions on origins and variant versions, but they have also provided what is almost a bibliographical supplement in the form of their *Three Centuries of Nursery Rhymes and Poetry for Children,* the catalogue of an exhibition held at the National Book League in 1973. An extended edition of that catalogue was published in a limited edition in 1977.

Beauty in the Enchanted Palace.

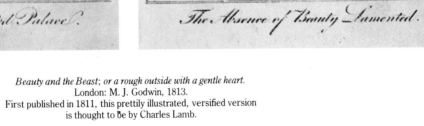

The Absence of Beauty Lamented.

*Beauty and the Beast; or a rough outside with a gentle heart.*
London: M. J. Godwin, 1813.
First published in 1811, this prettily illustrated, versified version
is thought to be by Charles Lamb.

*Tommy Thumb's Pretty Song-Book* of 1744 – they enjoy a precarious existence with an uncertain future. Very few of the nursery-rhyme books of the eighteenth century have survived and we can only make a sketchy estimate of the relationships between them. What can be said, however, is that *Tommy Thumb* set a pattern of deriving printed texts from spoken tradition, and that the books that followed it seem to respect its novelty in doing this.

We are hampered in gauging the full effect of *Tommy Thumb* on these later books because the 'Voll. I' that must have preceded the 'Voll. II' owned by the British Library has never been discovered. We do not know how many 'pretty songs' it adds to the twenty-nine in its companion volume, and we don't know what those songs are, but there are clear editorial and illustrative connections between what is found here and what is found in the other great eighteenth-century collection, *Mother Goose's Melody* (probably first published by Thomas Carnan and Francis Newbery in 1780 – and the book that brought the name 'Mother Goose' out of fairy-tales and into nursery rhymes.)[1]

Clues – still not completely followed up – are to be found in yet another rare book: what seems to be an abridged and re-edited piracy of *Tommy Thumb's Pretty Song-Book*, printed and published in Worcester, Massachusetts, by Isaiah Thomas in 1788. Round about that date Isaiah Thomas had suddenly launched a huge assault on the American children's book market by reprinting wholesale about fifty titles that were largely based on British originals, so it is entirely plausible that when he issued his own *Tommy Thumb's Song Book*, with a subtitle very close to Mary Cooper's, he was drawing upon her book or upon a now lost intermediate edition. From the thirty-four rhymes in his piracy we can hazard that at least nineteen may have come from the lost 'Voll. I', together with ten pages or so of animal pictures accompanied by transcriptions of appropriate animal noises: 'Bow Wow', etc.

Only three complete copies of this *Song Book* are recorded in the standard bibliography of early American children's books, and to these can be added a near-perfect copy of the second edition of 1794 in the Opie Collection. The rarity of this little paper-covered book, its fine condition, and its close relationship to the first-ever English collection of nursery rhymes point it up as being among the most delectable of all the Opie books. Alongside one other gem from the same period, *The Famous Tommy Thumb's Little Story-Book* (*c.*1760), which contains nine nursery rhymes, it makes an apt foundation for the expansive developments of later years.

One strand of these developments is the continual use of nursery rhymes as the basis for fairly substantial rhyme-books, often emphatically illustrated. The outburst of levity at the start of the nineteenth century produced a particularly long-lived example with *Songs for the Nursery* (1805), the first collection to have full-page illustrations and a notable influence on American rhyme books through its use in the making of a Boston edition of *Mother Goose's Melodies*.

As the nineteenth century progressed nursery rhymes became a completely accepted element in children's book publishing, and publishers and illustrators saw them (along with fairy-tales) as a natural, ready-made set of texts, unprotected by tiresome copyright prohibitions. The standard roster of

SONG BOOK. 41

CAT AND A FIDDLE.

HIGH Diddle, Diddle,
A Cat and a Fiddle ;
The Cow jump'd over the Moon :
The little Dog laugh'd
For to fee the Sport,
And the Difh ran after the Spoon.

*G I G A.*

COCK

*Tommy Thumb's Song Book for all Little Masters and Misses.* By Nurse Lovechild . . . the second Worcester edition. Printed at Worcester, Massachusetts by Isaiah Thomas, 1794. 100×66 mm.

The American nursery-rhyme piracy that helps us to build up evidence for what the first English nursery-rhyme book may have been like. 'Cat and Fiddle' does not appear in Vol. II of the English *Tommy Thumb*, but because of the way Isaiah Thomas dealt with it we may infer that it was one of the rhymes in Vol. I.

[1] Only one copy of this book has survived, too, dated 1791 and now in the Ball Collection in the Lilly Library at the University of Indiana. The Opie Collection can offer a battered, hand-coloured edition published by John Marshall in 1816, and even that seems to be the only one of its kind.

rhymes established in the period up to *Songs for the Nursery* was enhanced by such 'scholarly' collections as Joseph Ritson's *Gammer Garton's Garland* (published in its fullest form in 1810) and James Orchard Halliwell's pioneering *Nursery Rhymes of England* (1842), and from that time on the chief concern of editors seems to have been to plan the length and general design of their book and then throw in rhymes and pictures until everything fitted. 'Felix Summerly', alias Henry Cole, devised his 'Home Treasury' series of children's books in the mid-1840s: a uniform series intended to bring back elegance and good cheer to a genre that had temporarily become occluded by seriousness.[1] He naturally included *The Traditional Nursery Songs of England* (1843) – which Iona and Peter Opie claim to be the first rhyme book 'illustrated by artists of repute' – and the slightly stern formality of those artists' views of their chosen scenes contrasts oddly with the jumble of the verses, arranged in simple alphabetical order according to their first lines (see page 77).

Such casualness dominates the run of 'collected nursery rhyme books' down to the present time – the fat 'nursery editions', which often derived from Halliwell, being a case in point – and only rarely do editions turn up that seem to show close editorial control throughout. There is certainly a tradition of 'artistic' Mother Goose books, the first perhaps being Eleanor Vere Boyle's *Child's Play*, which began life as an experiment in anastatic printing and then became a sumptuous example of Victorian experimental colour printing; there was the effete, but technically brilliant *Mother Goose* of Kate Greenaway, and there were artsy-craftsy black-and-white designs in several *fin de siècle* books. But the collections that attain to something more than artistry or picturesqueness are those where – whatever the organization of the rhymes – the illustrator has captured something of the free, nonsensical imagination of the original rhyme-makers. Few nineteenth-century collections can match *The Old Nurse's Book of Rhymes, Jingles and Ditties* (1858), illustrated with drawings by Charles Bennett, whom the Opies reckon to be 'perhaps the first man to enter into the spirit of nursery rhymes', while Caldecott's skill in bringing a story alive in the rhymes was reflected in the black-and-white collection by his disciple, L. Leslie Brooke: *The Nursery Rhyme Book* (1897).

A second strand in the history of nursery-rhyme publishing has been the even more decidedly pictorial presentation of a single rhyme in a single book. *The Comic Adventures of Old Mother Hubbard* (1805) is something of a prototype here, emphasizing the practical consideration that a rhyme with a quantity of verses is likely to be a more suitable case for treatment in a book than a brisk narrative on the lines of,

> Charley Wag, Charley Wag
> Ate the pudding and left the bag.

Indeed, probably the first rhyme so to stand on its own was 'The House that Jack Built', in *Nurse Truelove's New-Year's Gift*, which John Newbery had printed round about 1750, and such was the length and adaptability of that rhyme that it often figured as a subject for individual chapbooks. (Another example which precedes *Mother Hubbard* is the doleful tale of *The Death and Burial of Cock Robin*. The Opie Collection has two copies of an edition printed at Lichfield by M.

*Nurse Truelove's New-Year's Gift.* London: at Newbery's and Carnan's, n.d. [?1765]. 84×55 mm.

Having at one time set himself high standards for collecting children's books complete and in good condition, Peter Opie later modified his views. He was delighted when he finally obtained this first printing of 'The House That Jack Built', even though it was in a shattered copy of the book, lacking a title-page.

[1] Incidentally, the Opie Collection includes various manuscript items associated with Cole, including his daughter's pocket-book and commonplace album.

Morgan, *c.*1797, one of them being in the form of the original printed sheet before it had been folded and cut to make a booklet.)

With single-rhyme picture-books the danger of the artist taking over to the detriment of 'the spirit of the rhymes' is at its most pronounced. Sarah Catherine Martin's quatrains for *Mother Hubbard* can't be said to possess a lot of spirit (it was the publisher who gave the book the momentum that kept it running), and they were not much enhanced by her stiff drawings, which missed most of the illustrative opportunities that her verses did offer; and that has tended to be the case ever since. Getting books on to the market has been the chief preoccupation of most children's book publishers, and the evolution of single-rhyme picture-books is more interesting for the light that it sheds on the history of graphic styles than for revelations of illustrative craftsmanship.

The 'Mother Hubbard' period was vivacious in its enthusiasm for picture-books – at first mostly printed from copper plates, later made up of letterpress texts printed with woodcut illustrations, and with a high frequency of hand-colouring. For almost forty years a great variety of such books poured from the presses, and the desk-drawers in 'Peter's Room' contained many witnesses to the popularity of individual nursery rhymes as themes for these books. The 'naturals' preponderate – *Cock Robin*, *The House that Jack Built*, and *Mother Hubbard* herself – and these are joined by those other rhyming catalogues that almost seem to have been designed to fit into the brief span of a chapbook: the alphabet rhymes *A Apple Pie* and *A was an Archer*.

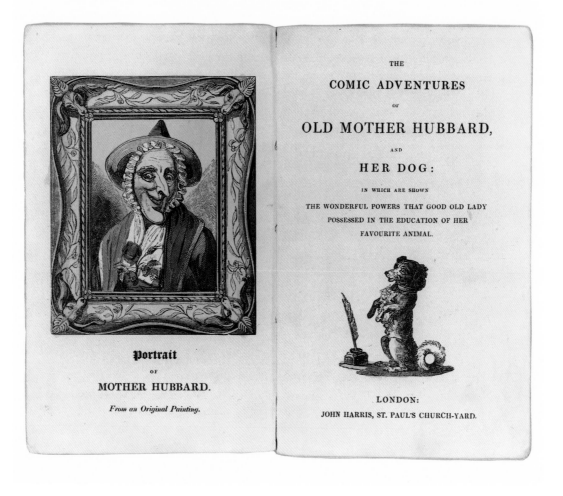

*The Comic Adventures of Old Mother Hubbard and her Dog.* London: John Harris, n.d. [1820].

With the success of his early picture-books, John Harris extended both the size and the number of later editions. Here is his refurbished edition of his first bestseller, now re-illustrated by Robert Cruikshank – and all the livelier for that. This example is not taken from a complete copy of the book, but from a portion which was bound up with parts of other Harris books, perhaps as a publisher's sample-book.

THE

COMIC ADVENTURES

OF

OLD MOTHER HUBBARD,

AND

HER DOG:

IN WHICH ARE SHOWN

THE WONDERFUL POWERS THAT GOOD OLD LADY
POSSESSED IN THE EDUCATION OF HER
FAVOURITE ANIMAL.

LONDON:
JOHN HARRIS, ST. PAUL'S CHURCH-YARD.

**Portrait**
OF
MOTHER HUBBARD.
*From an Original Painting.*

Nor did this conventional range of themes greatly alter when the hand-coloured books gave way to the larger picture-books of the second half of the nineteenth century, with their illustrations printed in colour, either from sets of wood-engraved blocks or from lithographic stones. Publishers began to exploit more fully the economies of series production, and the making of 'toy books' (as picture-books were then often called) became almost an industrial process. Routledge's 'New Sixpenny Toy Books' ran to nearly a hundred items between 1866 and 1889, and the rival 'Aunt Louisa' series from Frederick Warne & Co. ran to more than a hundred in roughly the same period.

Within the Routledge sixpenny series, however – and sometimes advertised as a quite separate series – were a group of picture-books that brought a strongly individual interpretation to the traditional texts: Walter Crane's 'Sixpenny Toy Books'. For Crane, who was a protean activist in arts-and-craftsmanship (turning out anything from bas-reliefs to trade-union banners at the drop of a golden guinea), struck up a collaboration with the colour printer Edmund Evans and between 1865 and 1876 turned out a regular two or three titles a year for his sixpenny picture-book series. This meant that he was always on the *qui vive* for themes that could be tailored into his standard sixteen pages, and we find him applying his inventive graphics to such single rhymes as *Sing a Song of Sixpence, One, Two, Buckle my Shoe,* and *This Little Pig Went to Market.* (See pages 84-85.)

The Opie Collection is very helpful in revealing the popularity of these toy books and in showing the different ways in which they were treated by the publisher to keep up with market trends. There are, all in all, forty-five copies of twenty-seven individual titles in Crane's sixpenny series, kept together to show variants in cover designs and advertisements, and, in addition, there are various bound books to show the publishers' habit of lumping several titles together and putting them out in a fancy binding for the gift-book trade. Several variant copies also exist of Crane's more imposing 'Shilling Series', first published by George Routledge and re-issued with a 'nineties look by John Lane at the Bodley Head.

In all probability Crane started this shilling series to try to get more financial gain for his work, since, by 1874 when the series began, he was a well-established illustrator. He was certainly put out when he heard about the terms arranged for a new nursery rhyme series that Edmund Evans was commissioning from a younger artist, Randolph Caldecott, who, shrewdly, had negotiated a commission on copies sold, and not a straight one-off payment of the kind that Crane had been getting. This series, the 'Randolph Caldecott Picture Books', was to come out at the rate of two titles a year over the eight years before Caldecott's early death in 1886, and the eventual sixteen titles have proved to be among the greatest felicities in English children's literature.

Like Crane, Caldecott did not depend wholly on nursery rhymes for his sources. He brought in ballads like *John Gilpin,* nonsense like *The Great Panjandrum Himself,* and even a traditional verse tale, *The Babes in the Wood,* but about half his texts may be found in the *Oxford Dictionary of Nursery Rhymes* and his treatment of these showed great skill in the matching of a pictorial narrative to the rhymes. Where Walter Crane tended to illustrate through a series of static, carefully composed pictures, Caldecott danced his way along, his set-piece scenes (often themselves full of wit and movement) being connected by a flow of intermediary drawings done in sepia which carried a story in themselves (see pages 88-89).

Iona and Peter Opie's own delight in Caldecott and their recognition of his pre-eminence as a 'nursery artist' ensured that his work was represented in the Collection at Westerfield by some rarities as well as by the standard works (and this is just as well, since American appreciation of Caldecott has much exceeded that accorded him by his fellow-countrymen, and large portions of surviving manuscript material, etc., are now in collections in the United States). Thus, alongside many variant editions of the 'Caldecott Picture Books' – some of which show a serious falling-off in the care and accuracy of printing that his work calls for – there were presentation copies of his books; there were holograph sketches; there was a small group of letters to William Allingham, one of which notes his forthcoming involvement with *John Gilpin*; and there were proofs for the covers and colour-plates for *Hey Diddle Diddle* and *The Milkmaid*, with the printed outline drawing coloured by Caldecott as a guide for the engraver of the colour blocks. Some of his comments, such as 'Moon to be lighter than ground. Ground to be rather grayer', remain in the margins.[1] (See page 123.)

The strength of the Nursery Rhyme Collection in representing major illustrators like Crane and Caldecott (and many lesser figures), and the depth

*A Christmas Box.* Bagatelles Set to Music by Mr Hook. London: printed and sold at A. Bland & Weller's, n.d. [1797]. 343×232 mm.

The earliest systematic publication of nursery rhymes with music.

[1]Because of their association with events in the life of the Opie family, all these Caldecott proofs have been retained at Westerfield.

of its holdings of rhyme-collections by no means exhaust its potential for demonstrating the special characteristics of children's literature as a genre. For just as important as the popularity of nursery rhymes as easy-come, easy-go subjects for collections and picture-books is the varied treatment that they receive from less orthodox or predictable points of view. From the very beginning, for instance, in *Tommy Thumb's* title, there was a recognition that these verses might be sung as well as recited, and it was much to the Opies' credit that they realized from the start that there was more to cheerful warbling than the printed word. Beginning with a run of James Hook's 'bagatelles for juvenile amusement' in *A Christmas Box* and its companions (1797–9), they sought to show the attempts made by publishers to put music to the traditional words, and although in the case of books like Walter Crane's *Baby's Opera* (1877) or Henriette Willebeek le Mair's *Our Old Nursery Rhymes* (1911) the music seems to be part of a larger decorative scheme, in instances like M.H. Mason's *Nursery Rhymes and Country Songs* (1878) there is an attempt to record traditional tunes 'in the field' as they were being sung.

In a less formal vein the Collection also represents the extent to which nursery rhymes have entered into the subconscious of the nation, or become a reference point from which a multitude of schemes may depart, secure in the knowledge that everyone will know the primal origin. Quite early in the nineteenth century 'The House that Jack Built' was being used on the one hand as the basis for a parlour game of forfeits, called *The Barn That Tom Built* (1817) and on the other as a theme for William Hone's satire on George II *The Political House that Jack Built* (1819), and from then on the field of reference widens until – as the Collection so brilliantly reveals – the rhymes became the great precursors of today's 'merchandising', appearing everywhere from matchbox labels to toilet-rolls.

At the same time they were being adapted to all the purposes that publishers and toy-makers might have beyond the simple reprinting of the verses in standard fashion. In 1857 *The Moveable Mother Hubbard* and the *Moveable Cock Robin* were put out by Dean & Son as the first of their books where pictures were given action by the pulling of a tab, preceding the pop-up book shown on page 39 by about six years. Thereafter almost every gimmick in the repertoire called upon nursery-rhyme themes at some point, whether for painting books and transfer pictures, or jigsaw puzzles and crosswords, fabric games and doll-dressing exercises. Considered in isolation, any such example could easily be taken with a shrug of the shoulders as only to be expected, but when seen on the scale brought about by these assiduous collectors even the dullest of ephemera given away with cornflakes takes on a peculiarly hallowed quality.

Perhaps the universality of nursery rhymes has been one of the leading reasons for the respect and affection in which the Opies' work has been held from the day that they published the *Dictionary* onwards – a general benevolence which has had the further effect of stimulating both the growth and the professionalism of the Collection as a resource. Not the least of the entertaining encounters brought about by the collectors' fame is mirrored in correspondence with Robert Graves and in Bernard Shaw's famous 'Opus

One', the rhyme that he made up for himself at an early age 'when petting our dog Rover':

> Dumpitty doodledum big bowwow
> Dumpitty doodledum dandy.

As Iona and Peter Opie say in the catalogue to their National Book League exhibition, that document can 'stand for the several thousand contributions which have been received over the years, and which are preserved in our archives'. The contributions may be recollected rhymes (some of which have recently been gathered by Iona Opie into the anthology *Tail Feathers from Mother Goose*) or mementos – not least Joan Hassall's gift of her scraper-board drawings for *The Oxford Book of Nursery Rhymes* – or additions to the Collection. Indeed, there is a pleasant symmetry in the fact that the enterprise that began with the purchase of *The Cheerful Warbler* ended, just before the Collection passed to the Bodleian, with the acquisition of Nicola Bayley's *Nursery Rhymes*, presented in variant editions by two admiring bibliographers and signed *in situ* by the artist.

*The Yellow Dwarf.*

*Mother Bunch's Fairy Tales.* Published for the amusement of all those little masters and misses who, by duty to their parents and obedience to their superiors, aim at becoming great lords and ladies. London: printed for E. Newbery, 1784.

The didactic sub-title rather undercuts the comfortable authorial designation 'Mother Bunch' – the publisher's name for the celebrated Mme D'Aulnoy. This Newbery collection was first published in 1773 and the twelve engravings in this edition may have been hand-coloured before publication.

*The Moveable Mother Hubbard.* London: Dean & Son, n.d. [c.1857]. 250×163 mm.

In its original state (now overcome by time and heavy use) the page would allow for dame and dog to bow to each other simultaneously on the pulling of the still-visible tab.

GRIMM'S GOBLINS.

BRUNILDA DISENCHANTS THE YELLOW DWARF, BY CUTTING OFF HIS BEARD.

spells, he has lengthened his life many hundred years; but his birth subjects him to death, which will be inevitable, should the infernal power by which he has accomplished his purposes be defeated. To prevent this catastrophe, he has placed his life on a talisman, which he believes unconquerable, but which, I trust, we shall overthrow. Caution is, however, necessary, for his spells are mighty, and the Spirits subjected to his command are many. In the interim, you shall rest here, and I will provide for your necessities till I

No. 25.

shall be able to conduct you to Brunilda, to whom you must explain the virtues of the Scissors of Fate; for, by an immutable decree which no Spirit dares violate, I am restrained from appearing before her till she herself shall summon me." The Gnome then raised a comfortable tent for Ludolph, loaded it with provisions, drew a line of protection about it, and vanished.

Three days passed tranquilly enough with Ludolph, while patiently awaiting the reappearance of his

193

*Grimms' Goblins*. London: George Vickers, n.d. [1861].
247×180 mm.

'The Yellow Dwarf' here forms one of the weekly parts of a Victorian fairy tale collection (not confined to stories by the Grimms) which was eventually bound up and sold as a book. Many of the illustrations were by 'Phiz' (Hablot Knight Browne), famous for his collaborations with Dickens. The colour printing, from woodblocks, is part of the experimental work of Edmund Evans.

The tale also figured among the numerous traditional subjects which Walter Crane used for his wide-ranging picture-book series:

*The Yellow Dwarf*. London, George Routledge & Sons, n.d. [1875] (Walter Crane's Toy Books).

After the elegancies of Regency illustration, fairy tales came to
be exploited with varying diversity by graphic artists:

An anonymous toy-book illustration for *Jack the Giant Killer*:
London, Routledge, n.d. [*c.*1872].

An attempt by the fastidious Hugh Thomson to use *Jack* to start
a 'Fairy Library': London, Macmillan & Co. Ltd., 1898.
212×180 mm. For reasons not readily apparent here, the
publisher abandoned the idea as 'too frightening'.

From a youthful manuscript of *Jack the Giant Killer* made by
Richard Doyle in 1842 and published in facsimile after his death:
London, Eyre & Spottiswoode, 1888. 247×195 mm.

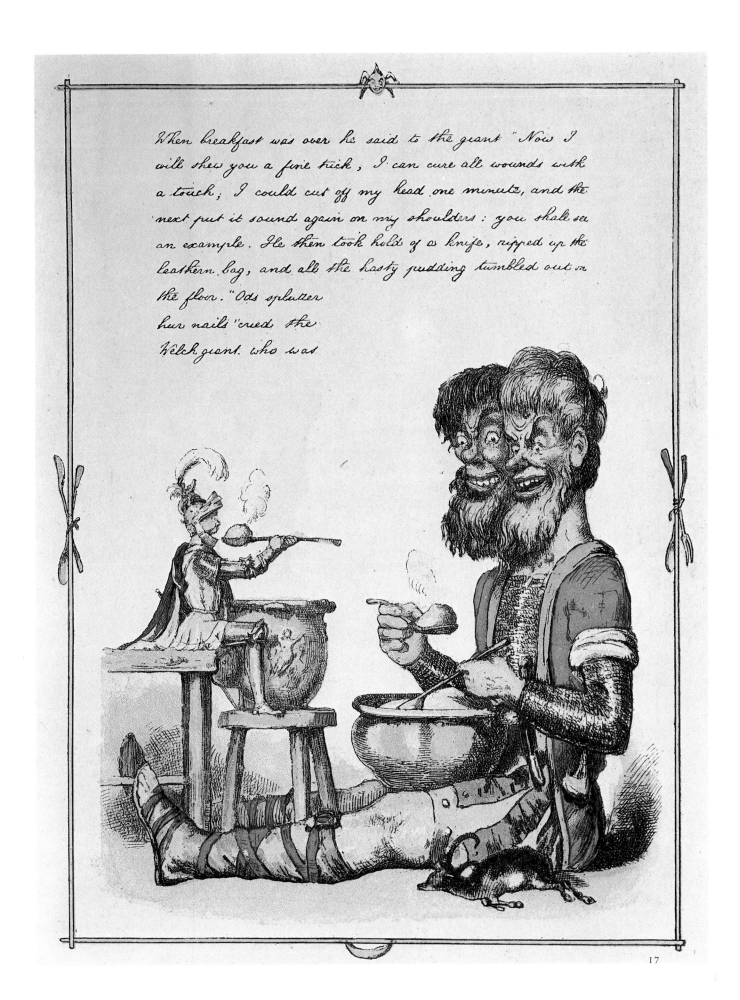

When breakfast was over he said to the giant "Now I
will shew you a fine trick, I can cure all wounds with
a touch; I could cut off my head one minute, and the
next put it sound again on my shoulders: you shall see
an example. He then took hold of a knife, ripped up the
leathern bag, and all the hasty pudding tumbled out on
the floor. "Ods splutter
hur nails "cried the
Welch giant, who was

*Mirth Without Mischief.* London: printed for C. Sheppard, n.d. [c.1780]. 103×64 mm.

A wonderful little compendium of entertainments, including the first printing of 'The Twelve Days of Christmas'. As may be guessed, 'Nimble Ned's Alphabet' has the letters constructed out of acrobatic figures.

FRONTISPIECE.

Here lads and lasses all repair,
And gather of this fruit so fair;
And those who gather most will find
'Twill make them wise and feed the mind,
And save them from the birch behind.

*Mirth without Mischief.*

COMTAINING

The Twelve Days of Christmas;
The Play of the Gaping-Wide-Mouthed-
Wadling Frog;
Love and Hatred;
The Art of Talking with the Fingers;
AND
Nimble Ned's Alphabet and Figures.

AT

School you must study your book for to
learn,
But when the school's over let mirth have
a turn.

LONDON:
Printed by J. Davenport, George's Court,
For C. SHEPPARD. No. 8, Aylesbury
Street, Clerkenwell.

[PRICE—THREE PENCE.]

*Children's Tales or Infant Prattle.* London: published Sept. 1818 by J. Bysh; sold by C. Penny. 94×89 mm.

One of the cheap, hand-coloured booklets produced for a popular market in the wake of *Songs for the Nursery.* Note that the nonsense rhyme 'Three children sliding' has been rationalized.

Little Jack a Dandy,
Lov'd plumb-cake, and sugar candy,
He bought some at a grocers shop,
And out he came, hop, hop, hop.

Some children slideing on the Ice,
All on a winters day,
The Ice gave way and three fell in,
The rest they ran away.

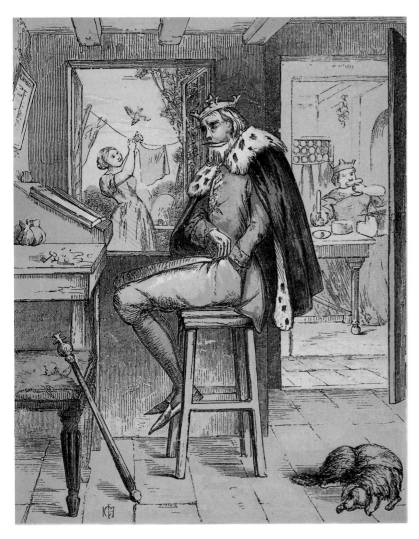

Left: *The Traditional Nursery Songs of England.*
With pictures by eminent modern artists.
Edited by Felix Summerly. London: Joseph Cundall, 1843.
(The Home Treasury series).

Consciousness of their eminence perhaps prevented
the artists from being too jocular with
their subject-matter. 'Sing a Song of Sixpence' is
about as jolly as they get.

Right: *Child's Play:* illustrated by E[leanor] V[ere] B[oyle].
London: Sampson Low, Son & Co., 1859. 190×145 mm.

A simple theme, but a complex bit of colour printing. Dickes
probably printed an outline plate in brown, and
then overlaid it with grained metal plates and/or woodblocks to
build up the colours.

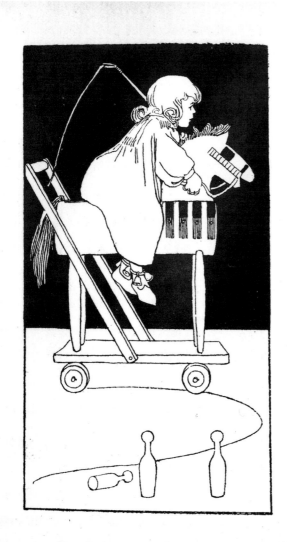

R IDE a cock-horse to Banbury Cross,
   To see a white lady ride on a
      white horse !
Rings on her fingers and bells on her
   toes,
And so she makes music wherever she
   goes.

*Banbury Cross and other nursery rhymes.* Illustrated by Alice
B. Woodward. London: J. M. Dent & Co., 1895, 146×90 mm.

*A Book of Nursery Songs and Rhymes.* With illustrations by members of the Birmingham Art School under the direction of A. J. Gaskin. London: Methuen, 1895. 22×133 mm.

Two examples of 'Ride a cock horse' filtered through an *art nouveau* lens. In the first there has been a mild infusion of Greenaway; in the second William Morris and the Kelmscott Press loom heavily over the page.

RIDE a cock-horse
    to Banbury Cross,
To see an old woman
    ride on a white horse;
With rings on her fin-
    gers and bells on her
    toes,
She shall have music
    wherever she goes.

KISS IN THE RING.

[*This popular game is honored with a variety of jingles, but generally commencing—*]

SALLY, Sally Waters, sprinkle in the pan,
    Hie, Sally! Hie, Sally, for a young man!
        Choose for the best,
        Choose for the worst,
   Choose for the prettiest that you love best.

( 35 )

Left: *The Old Nurse's Book of Rhymes, Jingles and Ditties.* Edited and illustrated by Charles H. Bennett. London: Griffith & Farran, 1858.

Unlike Felix Summerly's 'eminent artists', Charles Bennett knew what was needed: 'perhaps the first man to enter into the spirit of nursery rhymes', said Peter Opie.

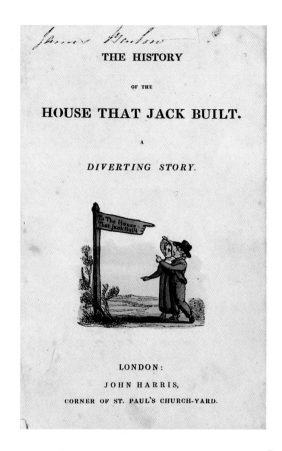

THE HISTORY

OF THE

HOUSE THAT JACK BUILT.

A

DIVERTING STORY.

LONDON:

JOHN HARRIS,

CORNER OF ST. PAUL'S CHURCH-YARD.

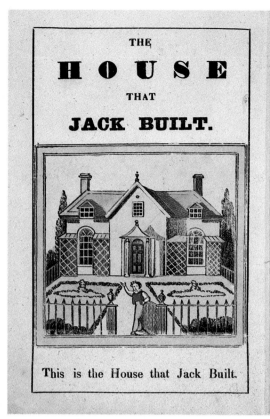

THE

HOUSE

THAT

JACK BUILT.

This is the House that Jack Built.

Three stages in the development of nursery rhyme real estate:

*The History of the House that Jack Built.* London: John Harris, n.d. [1819]. 167×104 mm.

*The House that Jack Built.* No publisher, n.d. [1830] 183×123 mm. Part of an anonymous uncut sheet, hand-coloured but not yet put into covers.

*The House that Jack Built.* Drawn by 'The Pilgrims'. London: Anthony Treherne & Co. Ltd., n.d. [*c.* 1905]. Approx. 38×153 mm.

A 'Stump Book', gimmicky in format, but still doing justice to the popular rhyme. When not being read, the book's pages were held in place by a peg at the outer edge.

THE
*Tragical Death*
OF A
*APPLE-PYE,*
WHO WAS
*Cut in Pieces and Eat by*
Twenty Five Gentlemen
WITH WHOM
ALL LITTLE PEOPLE
OUGHT
*To be very well acquainted*

Printed by John Evans,
42, Long-lane, West-smith-
field, London

Three servings of an Apple Pie.
Three examples of a traditional text, showing its transition
from small eighteenth-century chapbook to large-format
Victorian classic:

*The Tragical Death of a Apple-Pye.* London: printed by John
Evans. n.d. [1791]. 94×58 mm.

*A Apple Pie*; illustrated by Kate Greenaway. London: George
Routledge & Sons. n.d. [1886]. 217×265 mm.

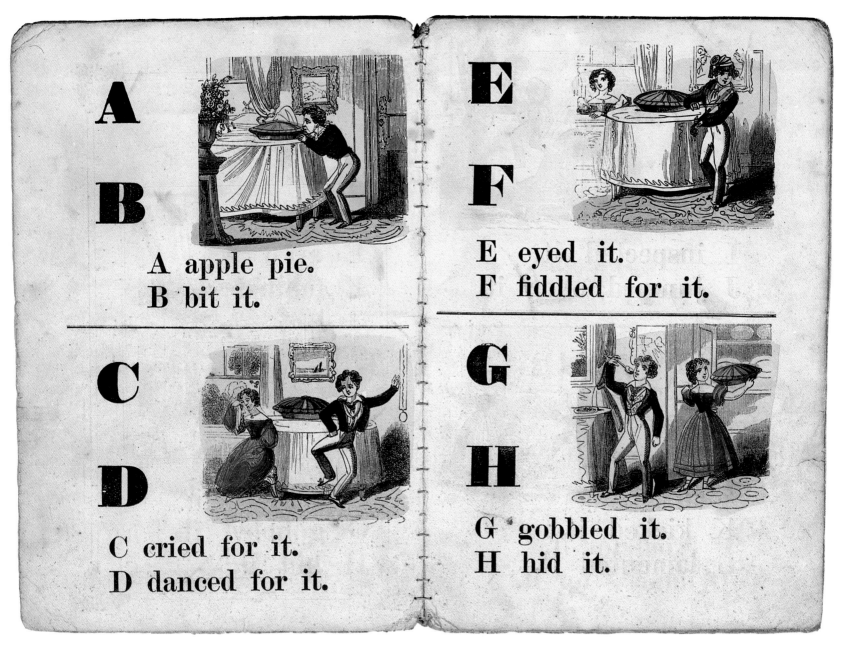

**A** apple pie.
**B** bit it.

**C** cried for it.
**D** danced for it.

**E** eyed it.
**F** fiddled for it.

**G** gobbled it.
**H** hid it.

*Darton's Indestructible Apple Pie.* London: Darton & Co.
n.d. [*c.* 1860]. 250×175 mm.

The pie was not indestructible, but the book was intended
to be so, being printed on linen.

*The Song of Sixpence Picture Book*;
with twenty-four pages of illustrations by Walter Crane. London:
George Routledge & Sons, n.d. [1876]. 250×190 mm.

*Sing a Song of Sixpence.*
London etc., Frederick Warne & Co., n.d. [*c.* 1875].
255×194 mm.

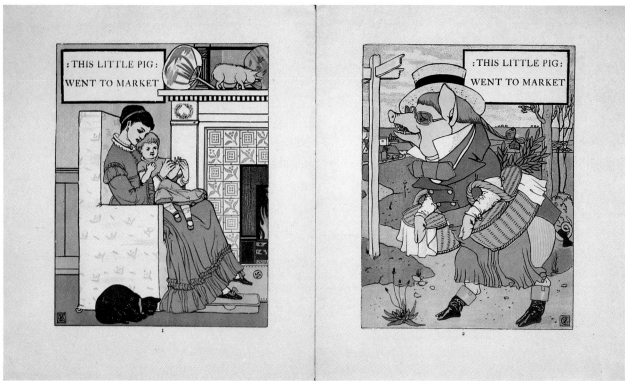

One of Crane's earliest picture-books – completely free and easy
– contrasted with his later, heavier, more imposing style:

*Sing a Song of Sixpence.* Designed by Walter Crane. London:
George Routledge & Sons, n.d. [*c.*1876]. 244×186 mm. First
published in 1866.

*This Little Pig Went to Market.* Illustrated by Walter Crane.
London: George Routledge & Sons, n.d. [1871]. (Routledge's
'New Sixpenny Toy Books'). 242×185 mm.

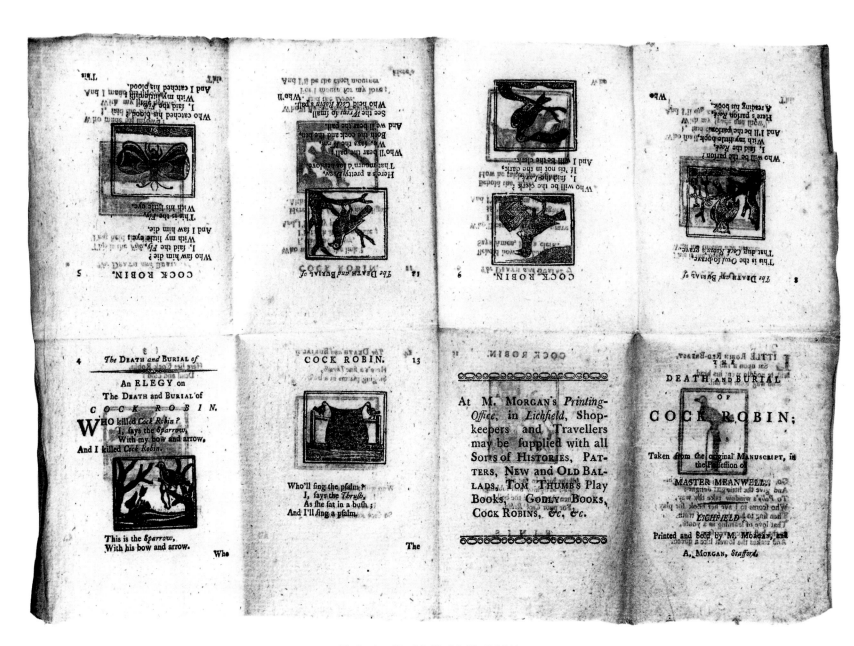

*The Death and Burial of Cock Robin.* Lichfield:
printed and sold by M. Morgan and A. Morgan [at] Stafford,
n.d. [*c.*1797]. Size of sheet: 217×318 mm.

*Cock Robin* before he was sold to the
citizens of Lichfield and the world: a sheet printed on both sides,
ready for folding and stitching to make up a simple chapbook.

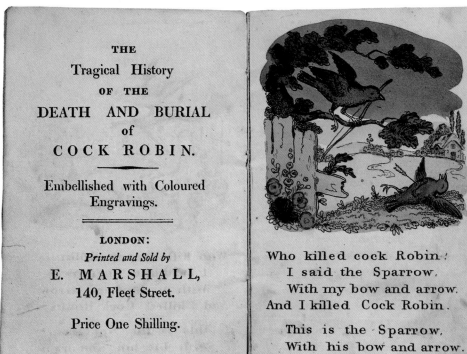

THE
Tragical History
OF THE
DEATH AND BURIAL
of
COCK ROBIN.

Embellished with Coloured
Engravings.

LONDON:
*Printed and Sold by*
E. MARSHALL,
140, Fleet Street.

Price One Shilling.

Who killed cock Robin?
I said the Sparrow.
With my bow and arrow.
And I killed Cock Robin.

This is the Sparrow.
With his bow and arrow.

*The Death and Burial of Cock Robin.*
London: W. Darton. n.d. [?1813] 120×195 mm.

For its day, a handsome coloured edition, contrasting strongly
with the crudities of Mr Morgan of Lichfield's chapbook.

*The Tragical History . . . of Cock Robin.*
London: printed and sold by E. Marshall, n.d. [1823].
152×99 mm.

A brightly got-up copy of a tragical history.
The book was published by John Marshall's widow and has
all the characteristics of his 'late' style:
speckled boards, a pretty label, and bags of gaudy colouring.

A collection of covers designed by Randolph Caldecott for his
Shilling Picture Books. Their lightness and sense of movement
contrasts strongly with Crane's solid patterning in *This Little Pig
Went to Market* (above).

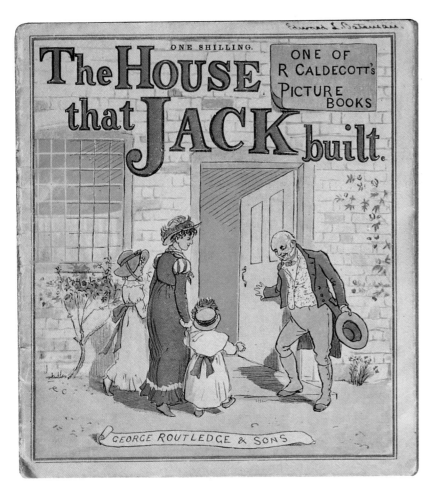

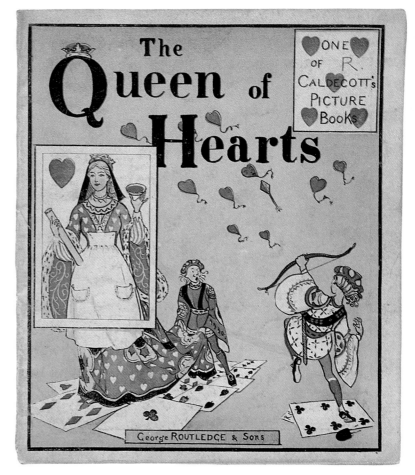

*The Baby's Opera;* a book of old rhymes with new dresses, by Walter Crane. London: George Routledge & Sons, n.d. [1877]. 182×187 mm.

Walter Crane's application of pictorial surrounds to a musical setting. Shown alongside is Crane's original water-colour design for the full-page picture. This would have been engraved on wood as seen here and would thus have printed as a mirror-image.

*Lullabies and Night Songs.* Music by Alec Wilder. Edited by
William Engvick. Pictures by Maurice Sendak. New York:
Harper & Row, 1965. 330×242 mm.

Perhaps the most original and varied of all the musical collections
of nursery verse. The Opie copy carries a greeting from the
illustrator, depicting a satisfied intruder from the land where the
wild things are.

91

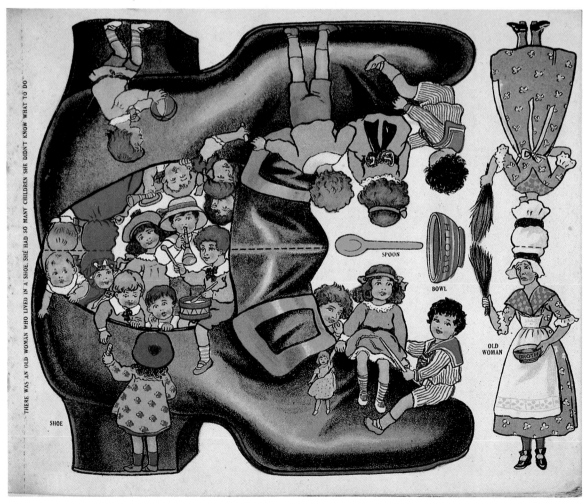

Three examples of the commercial exploitation of nursery rhymes:

*Nurseryland.* London: Raphael Tuck & Sons, n.d. [*c.*1914] (Father Tuck's 'Little Builders' Paper Modelling Series 3). 218×273 mm.

*The 'Nursery Rhyme' Pictorial Reading and Writing Cards.* London & Glasgow: Charles & Son Ltd. n.d. [1918]. Box size: 117×169×15 mm.

*Ten Little Nursery Rhymes* [seen as though in a television set] illus. Dinah. London: Raphael Tuck & Son, n.d. [1953]. 249×197 mm.

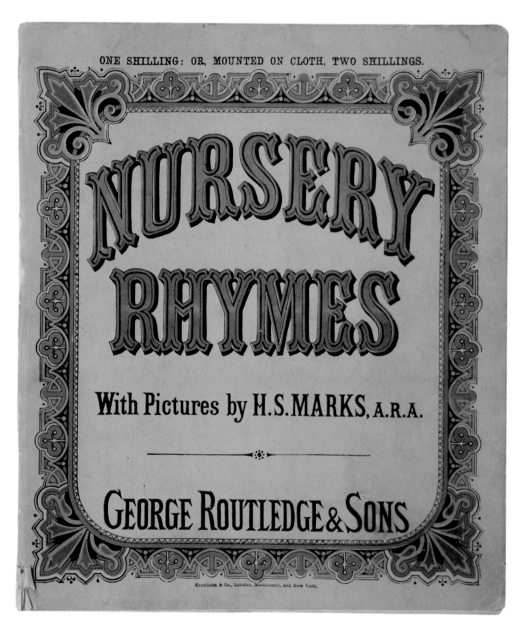

*Nursery Rhymes*; illustrated by Stacey Marks. London: George
Routledge & Sons. n.d. [*c.*1865] (Routledge's 'Shilling Toy
Books' No. 1). 265×229 mm.

One of Routledge's brilliant fairground covers for a new series of
picture-books that was to be among the most popular of its time.

*Nicola Bayley's Book of Nursery Rhymes.*
London: Jonathan Cape, 1975.

The same. Harmondsworth: Puffin Books, 1975.

Nicola Bayley's first book appeared, to much acclaim, with the
elegant cover seen above. A reprint was quickly called for; the
printing was moved from Britain to Italy; and a new 'popular'
cover was designed. This – however out of keeping with the
book's artistic style – was retained for later editions, including
the Puffin paperback shown here.

# CLASSICS IN CONTEXT

Fairy-tales and nursery rhymes may not have won for themselves an entirely enthusiastic reception among those who held the purse-strings of the eighteenth century – cultural and fiscal alike. Looking back on their emergence now, however, we can see that texts like Perrault's *Histories* and Mother Goose's *Melodies* are almost the only works published for children that have survived more or less unchanged to the present time. Of the hundreds of books written by authors 'for the instruction and amusement of Little Master Tommy and Pretty Miss Polly' scarcely a word remains current. The thin strain of amusement could not sufficiently dilute the turbid instruction.

Here and there, chiefly in poetry, echoes persist. There are still adults to be found who recall with pleasure (influenced by nostalgia?) the reading or singing of some of Isaac Watts's *Divine Songs Attempted in Easy Language for the Use of Children*, first published in 1715, and remaining in print till the twentieth century. And two poems from that work ('How doth the little busy bee' and ''Tis the voice of the sluggard') are now immortalized through their parodies in *Alice's Adventures in Wonderland*.

Watts too is present as an influence on poets of larger stature: Christopher Smart, protégé of John Newbery (and brother-in-law of his manager Thomas Carnan), and William Blake. Smart, however, never quite found a voice for children's poetry, while Blake, who did , and who in doing so produced the one masterpiece of eighteenth-century children's literature, was unknown to his

*The Children of the New Forest.* By Capt. Marryat, R.N. In two vols. London: H. Hurst, n.d. [1847]. 166×103 mm.

One of the engravings designed for the first volume of the first edition by Marryat's son Frank. The book has claim to be the earliest English children's novel to remain continuously in print down to the present day.

*Children of the Forest at the Grave of Jacob Armitage*

times. The first edition of *Songs of Innocence* published for children, rather than connoisseurs of Blake, appeared in 1899, 110 years after Blake's own edition.

So far as stories are concerned, the eighteenth-century books that children may have read and that still have life in them are works written for adults, such as *The Life and Strange Surprizing Adventures of Robinson Crusoe* (1719) and *Travels into Several Remote Nations of the World* by Lemuel Gulliver (1728). Here were tales where the power to amuse easily outran instructive undercurrents, and where the nineteenth-century writers for children were to find much scope for their inventive powers. For although the beginning of that century had produced one storyteller of near-genius, Maria Edgeworth, and a family of writers of great character, 'the Taylors of Ongar', their best work was embedded in its period. Some stories from *The Parent's Assistant* (1796) have been reprinted for children in modern times, some verses from *Original Poems for Infant Minds* (1804–5) still crop up in anthologies (and, indeed, like the two Watts poems, 'Twinkle, twinkle, little star' from *Rhymes for the Nursery* is remembered via *Alice*), but the first complete book to survive more or less to the present is Johann Wyss's Crusoe-inspired farrago *The Swiss Family Robinson*.

Accusations could be made that it is cheating to call *The Swiss Family Robinson* the longest-lived classic story, since like *Tales from Shakespear* retold by Charles and Mary Lamb (1806) it owes its inspiration to other people's texts – not just Defoe, but also the German Joachim Heinrich Campe, who wrote an immensely successful Rousseauist version of *Robinson Crusoe* for children. Moreover, a sizeable proportion of Wyss's book that we know in later editions did not come from him, or from Switzerland, at all, but from a French expansion of the story by Mme Montholieu. Nevertheless, the transference of exotic adventure from adult books to children's books was a significant event, and *The Swiss Family Robinson*, as well as maintaining its own place as a 'classic story', directly moved Frederick Marryat to competition and may be said to lie behind not just *Masterman Ready* (1841–2) but also *The Children of the New Forest* (1847) and *The Little Savage* (1848–9).

The jump in dates from the Wyss of 1814 to the Marryat of the 1840s is not quite the random gap that it may seem. For after the euphoria of experimentation that came with that first decade of the next century, the publishers of children's books seem to have lost their nerve or to have settled down to consolidate their gains. With few exceptions – like the momentous arrival of the Brothers Grimm in English with *German Popular Stories* (1823–6) – the world of children's books maintained an air of decorous worthiness that lasted through the 1820s and 1830s.

The chances are that the children themselves would not have recognized this (or most of the adults who supplied them, who would doubtless reiterate what every generation says: 'We didn't have books like that when *I* was

38 DIVINE SONGS

SONG XV.

*Against Lying.*

O 'Tis a lovely Thing for Youth
To walk betimes in Wisdom's Way;
To fear a Lie, to speak the Truth,
That we may trust to all they say.

*Dr Watts's Divine and Moral Songs for Children;* revised and altered so as to render them of general use. London: printed by permission of the proprietors, for J. Johnson, 1787. 95×85 mm.

Although first published in 1715, Watts's *Divine Songs* long remained in plain text. Johnson's edition of 1787 is the earliest known dated edition to contain illustrations – some of which forcefully comment on the Doctor's divine sentiments.

young'). Our perception today comes through being able to chart the extraordinary upswing in the activity of publishers and in the variety of books that they produced during the progress of the 1840s, when roots were established for the ramifying developments of the Victorian period.

Year in, year out, as the century progressed, more and more books were produced for a widening market. Advances in the technologies of both printing and binding permitted faster print-runs, a multiplicity of page-formats and elaborate variations in the design and colouring of books. The reciprocation between producer and consumer stimulated quests for creative satisfaction – or for a comfortable living – from the writers, the artists and the hacks.

This growing momentum in the book industry (which has scarcely slowed down in all the years down to the present) is a feature which should loom large for the collector of children's books. For one thing it provided a degree of economic buoyancy which enabled experimentation to take place, and for another it supported a pattern of production within which important contributions could be nurtured. Recognition of such factors was an essential part of Iona and Peter Opie's philosophy in building up the Opie Collection of Children's Literature, and the thousands of comparatively run-of-the-mill books dating from the 1840s onward form a vital context to their holdings of books which are of historic significance.

We need to look at only two books from the momentous 1840s to see what this implies. The first – one of the most remarkable in the whole of English children's literature – is Edward Lear's *A Book of Nonsense*, as published by 'Derry Down Derry' (who loved to see little folks merry) in two volumes in 1846. Received wisdom holds that the importance of this book lies in its totally uninhibited commitment to its subject. By combining the ridiculous limerick stanzas with daft drawings, Lear brought a new freedom to the stuffy world of children's books. At the same time, though, the book represents something in the way of a technical experiment, since it was printed lithographically, with Lear himself probably preparing the images on the stones.

In these respects *A Book of Nonsense* stands in sharp contrast to the conventional books of its time, against whose dull rationalism Henry Cole (alias 'Felix Summerly') had also been inveighing. His 'Home Treasury' series was one of the harbingers of a new attitude both to traditional stories and to book-production standards – different from, but in the same climate as Edward Lear's; and if *Nonsense* symbolizes a new freedom for writers, alongside Cole's freer promulgation of traditional tales, then so too does the publication in 1846 of the first translations of Hans Christian Andersen, earliest and greatest of those writers for children who harnessed the tradition of the fantastic tale to their own purposes.

The second book which is full of consequence for its period is the *Struwwelpeter* of Heinrich Hoffmann, which was first published in Frankfurt in 1845 and was there, after translation, manufactured for import to England in 1848. (As in *A Book of Nonsense*, the author's drawings were lithographed, but the book was then coloured by hand.) Controversy has long flourished over whether Hoffmann intended his collection of cautionary stories to be admonitory or satirical – and if the latter is the case, then the book stands as a

They raise to Heaven the voice of song.          E

*The Songs of Innocence* by William Blake; with designs by Celia Levetus. London: Wells Gardner, Darton & Co., 1899. 72×56 mm.

Kate Greenaway is (inappropriately) echoed in this miniature edition of Blake's *Songs*, which is probably the first to be published for children since his own obscure edition of 1789.

very early example of a writer for children sending up the shibboleths of his time. But even if one leaves aside such a tempting interpretation, *Struwwelpeter* still remains first a revolutionary example of book illustration, and second a work of enormous influence among English book-producers.

Iona and Peter Opie were quick to recognize these characteristics, and their Struwwelpeter books and items form something of a collection within the Collection. Not only did they acquire the exceptionally rare first English edition, but they supported it with extensive purchases, including half a dozen variant copies up to the ninth edition, about twenty-six later variants (plus two with musical arrangements), several early German editions, and about forty imitations and parodies. These attest not only the popularity of Hoffmann's original (many of the examples show signs of heavy use), but also the immense adaptability of both his themes and his graphic ideas, with their recourse to composite narrative (i.e. a sequence of events compounded within a single picture), to primitive strip cartoon, and to symbolic decorations: with, for instance, birch-rods forming part of the frame to the illustration of Fidgetty Phil pulling down the table-cloth. Furthermore, it is arguable that by using a larger page size so successfully he paved the way for the adoption of the large-format picture books which were to become so popular in the second half of the century.

*A Book of Nonsense*; by 'Derry Down Derry' [i.e. Edward Lear] 2 vols. London: Thos. MacLean, 1846. 144×210 mm.

The hand-lithographed title-page for one of the most important children's books ever published. It appeared in two volumes, with each plate separately bound in. In consequence the books have often split into two – or more – pieces (like the Old Man of Nepaul, who 'from his horse had a terrible fall').

A recent census of known copies shows that only six complete, and more or less perfect, sets of the first edition are known, and of these 'Opie' appears to be the finest.

There was an old Derry down Derry,
Who loved to see little folks merry:
So he made them a Book,
And with laughter they shook,
At the fun of that Derry down Derry!

Published, Feb. 10. 1846, by Thos. McLean, 26, Haymarket.

This was the period during which the concept of 'classic books for children' took on the meaning which it has possessed ever since and during which many of the most famous (or notorious) examples were published. These are the 'treasures' that will be immediately recognizable to an audience who might otherwise be slightly mystified by the holy awe engendered by battered copies of *A Token for Children* or unillustrated primers like *A Child's Week's Work*. These are the achievements that justify everything else.

True to form, the Opie Collection has refined that view. It does indeed include most of the acknowledged 'classics' in a first or a very early edition – bringing home the force of one collector's admirable justification for buying first editions: the peculiar *frisson* to be gained from owning an important work of literature in its earliest form. Going one step further, though, the Opies have sought out books in outstanding condition or books that are the 'individual copies' that Peter so liked. Thus although they do not come close to a pristine *Alice* – their copy of the 1866 edition is in a very unhappy state – they do have *Through the Looking Glass* (1872) with a presentation inscription by Dodgson to one of the Harman children, together with a *Nursery Alice* (1890) inscribed 'to Coventry Patmore from the author'. Among other 'association' copies there is a first edition of *Black Beauty* (1877) – very rare in any state – inscribed by Anna Sewell; there is the play edition of *Peter Pan* (1928) given by J. M. Barrie to Nannie Falkner, nurse to the Lost Boys; there are two Kate Greenaways given 'to Eddie from his aunt Kittie'; and there is a clutch of volumes signed by A. A. Milne and E. H. Shepard, sometimes both together. A Japanese translation of *The House at Pooh Corner,* given to the Opies by A. A. Milne, includes his handwritten comic apology: 'For the Opie Collection – all my own work (except the misprint on p. 170).'

Presentation copies and the like have a natural tendency to live less rumbustious lives than plain copies sold over the counter for cash, without any distinguished associations, and there is thus a special glamour about those ordinary books that have been cared for and have survived in something close to their original condition. The Opie Collection has some remarkable examples of books from the last decades of the nineteenth century and the first decades of this which have been preserved in almost pristine state because they have been kept in their original dust-wrappers. The survival of the paper wrappers themselves is matter for wonder, but when they have conserved the freshness of the covers of such books as H. H. Emmerson's Greenaway-esque *The May Blossom* (*c.*1882) and E. Nesbit's *Railway Children* (1906) there is occasion for double rejoicing. Of all the fine copies of modern books in the Collection, though, the most perfect are surely the amazing run of Beatrix Potters – headed by mint copies of the two books which were published privately before being taken up by the trade: *The Tale of Peter Rabbit* (1901) and *The Tailor of Gloucester* (1902). These are followed by a succession of fine copies of the trade editions, capped by a reprint of *The Tale of Little Pig Robinson* (1930), signed by Beatrix Potter, and a copy of *The Fairy Caravan* (1929) specially made up to secure copyright in the English market. (The book was first published in the United States, and Beatrix Potter had no desire for it to appear in England, feeling that it was 'too personal', but a hundred copies

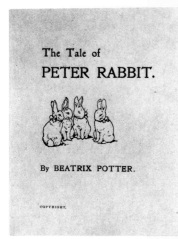

*The Tale of Peter Rabbit.* By Beatrix Potter. Copyright. [London: privately printed, 1901.] 135×103 mm.

The front cover of *Peter Rabbit*'s first appearance in book form. Beatrix Potter had 250 copies printed, some of which she gave away and some of which she sold at a price of 1*s.* 2*d.* Such was its success that she ordered another 200 copies with a title-page date of 1902 before Frederick Warne's could get a trade edition in print.

were prepared with different preliminary pages and were registered here to prevent piracy.)

Despite such rarities – and not forgetting the thrill that goes with owning important first editions – there remains a need to pay homage to those large portions of the Opie Collection which have no apparent distinction but which contain 'treasures' of a more obscure kind. For although the Classics may be sanctioned as such by virtue of their salient qualities or through a kind of unthinking inertia – adults passing on well-known slabs of prose to their children, or publishers preserving famous titles in a standard 'library' – there are also those books which an individual child may have come across and made his own for the space of a single childhood. We have no means of telling what will govern such personal choices. They are dependent for each of us upon unique circumstances: opening a Christmas stocking at *that* moment, unearthing (all by oneself) *that* book in *that* corner of some old Carnegie Library. What matters though is the affection engendered by such discoveries, and any collection that seeks to take account of Child Life as well as Children's Literature must make room for cartloads of apparent dross, in the awareness that this may have figured more prominently in the experience of many readers than the august works that everyone believes the same readers should have been consuming.

The Opie holdings of Victorian picture-books are a case in point here: box after box in the Knaster Room revealing the inventiveness, or merely the dogged perseverance, that publishers devoted to sustaining their series of 'Uncle Buncle' or 'Aunt Euphemia' titles. And where story-books are concerned, such is the growing sentiment today for ancient copies of the anything-but-classic Enid Blyton, that it is not difficult to comprehend the significance of shelves lined with equivalent products of the past: the Hentys and the Angela Brazils that were the consolation of the grandparents and great-grandparents of today's young.

Of special interest among such popular works are the multitudinous children's periodicals, which have no modern equivalent. Very much the creation of the Victorian period – and a form of speculation that led to occasional successes and frequent failures – the periodical proved to be a meeting-ground for all varieties of and attitudes to writing for children. Within the earnest, but not unattractive, pages of *Good Words for the Young* (1869–77) there appeared the major fantasies of George MacDonald, accompanied by the superlative drawings of Arthur Hughes. Mrs Ewing, in her mother's and her own *Aunt Judy's Magazine* (1866–85), published most of her finest stories and encouraged contributions from such as Hans Christian Andersen, Lewis Carroll and Randolph Caldecott. The almost entirely insignificant *Young Folks* (1876–97) took on a serial called 'The Sea Cook', which turned into *Treasure Island*. And on the other side of the Atlantic, in the pages of *St Nicholas* (1873–1940), Mary Mapes Dodge was creating a kind of bedrock of assurance which would allow the children's literature of the United States to gather its own confidence.

Almost all issues of all these magazines are present in the Opie Collection, even though they mostly exist in the bound-up volumes that publishers put out as Christmas annuals. They subsist alongside the entirely populist – if not scandalous – numbers of such 'bloods' as *The Boys of England,* where Jack Harkaway made his appearance, and among the penny-number novelettes and the early comics, which have proved to be the longest-lasting species of English periodical publication. And it was in apt recognition of that fact that the Opies sought to master a technique for adding comics to the Collection without causing Westerfield House to sink into the ground. The complete representations of popular papers in print on one specific day, repeated at ten-year intervals, at least allowed for a sketch of the evolution of the fashion in comics; and by coupling this to extensive holdings of some titles, like *Rainbow* and *Eagle,* and by building a file of children's opinions about their comics, a base was established for exploring the peculiar fascination of 'modern street literature'. (See pages 116–117.)

A vast gulf may appear to be fixed between John Newbery's *Lilliputian Magazine* and today's *Beano,* or indeed between the cramped bigotry of *A Token for Children* and the free fabling of *Just So Stories* or *The Wind in the Willows*; but it is not an unbridgeable gulf, and the wide span and the filigree tracery that is the Opie Collection of Children's Literature shows majestically the traditions and interconnections of the whole.

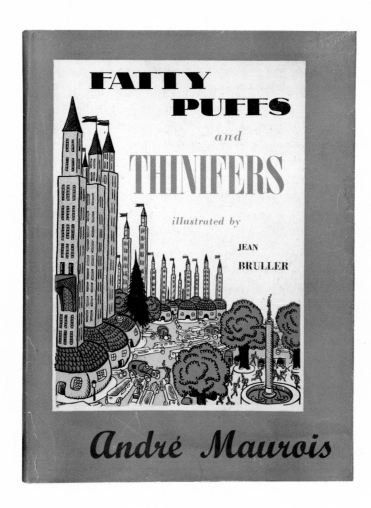

*Fattypuffs and Thinifers.* By André Maurois; illustrated by Jean Bruller. London: John Lane, 1941.

The pristine dust-jacket on a more recent children's book – but perhaps as scarce in this condition as the covers of earlier examples. The artist Jean Bruller was later to win fame as 'Vercors', the author of *Le Silence de la Mer.*

*Original Poems for Infant Minds.* By several young persons. London: printed and sold by Darton and Harvey, 1804. 130×80 mm.

The frontispiece and title-page of the first edition – a notoriously rare book, whose acquisition brought much joy to Westerfield.

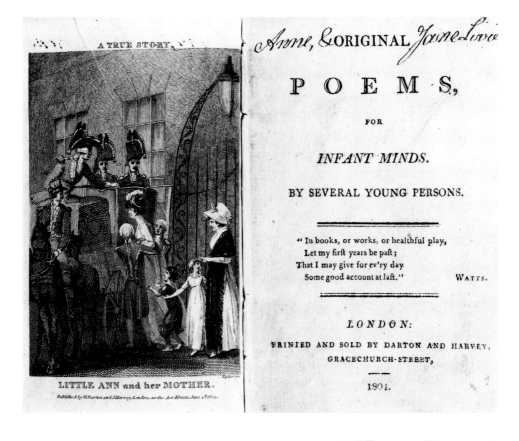

*The Family Robinson Crusoe* translated from the German of M. Wiss. Vol. II. London: printed for M. J. Godwin & Co, 1816. 175×98 mm. [chart = 175×195 mm.]

The *Swiss Family Robinson* has a complicated printing history – made more so by the scarcity of examples.

It first appeared in two volumes (as *The Family Robinson Crusoe*) in 1814, and these two volumes were reprinted as a single volume the same year. Then, in 1816, this one volume was added to by a second containing 'further adventures' and including the chart shown here. Only in 1818 was the title changed to the one we all know.

The Opie Collection has an almost complete representation of all these early editions.

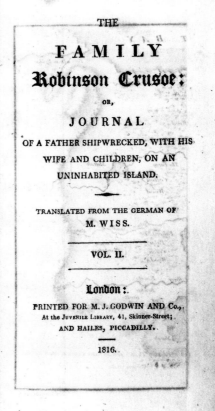

*Nursery Rhymes*; illustrated by Alfred Crowquill.
London: T. Nelson & Sons, n.d. [1864] (Nelson's Oil Colour
Picture Books for the Nursery). 269×230 mm.

'Alfred Crowquill' [i.e. A. H. Forrester] was one of the most
prolific of the early picture-book artists
who adopted a larger 'Struwwelpeter' format for their work.

*The English Struwwelpeter; or pretty stories and
funny pictures for little children.*
After the sixth edition of the celebrated German work of
Dr Heinrich Hoffmann. Leipzig: Friedrich Volckmar; London: at
the Agency of the German Literary Society, n.d. [1848].

'Shock-headed Peter' in his first manifestation, before Hoffmann
drew the better-known, more stylized version. The pictures
were lithographed and hand-coloured in Germany for the English
market. In 1973, Peter Opie claimed that fewer than six perfect
copies of the first English edition were known.

A group of books showing changes in the treatment of the original text of *Struwwelpeter*, mostly by imitation and parody:

*The Book of Bosh*: with which are incorporated some amusing and instructive nursery stories in rhyme. London: Griffith, Farran, Okeden & Welsh, 1889. 285×123 mm.

A work combining influences from Hoffmann (cautionary verses) and Edward Lear (the title, and some rather feeble limericks). The publishers advertised themselves as being in direct line of succession from the firms of Newbery and John Harris.

*Lazy Bones, or funny rhymes with funny pictures*. London: Routledge, Warne & Routledge, n.d. [c.1860]. 217×166 mm.

Another imitation, devoted entirely to the decline and fall of a lazy boy.

*Petrol Peter*. By Archibald Williams, illustrated by A. Wallis Mills. London: Methuen & Co., n.d. [1906]. 290×200 mm.

A parody of Hoffmann's text adapted to age of the car.

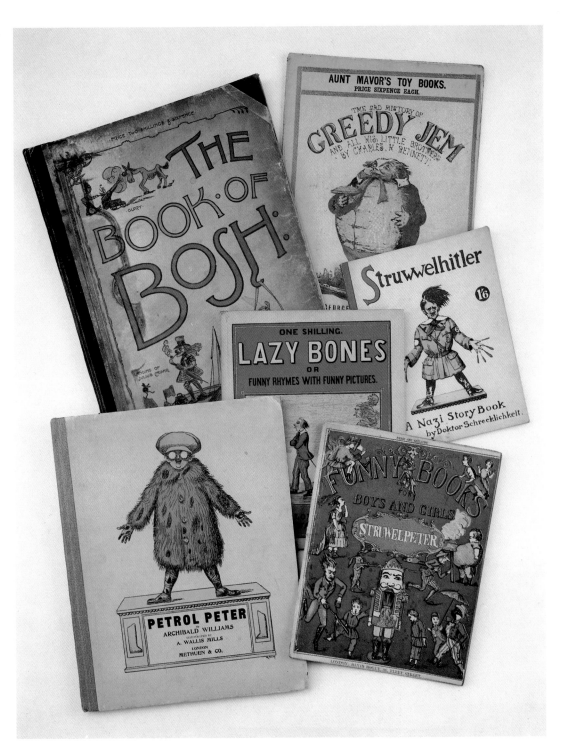

*The Sad History of Greedy Jem*, narrated, invented and drawn on the wood by Charles H. Bennett. London: Routledge, n.d. [1858] (Aunt Mavor's Toy Books). 242×180 mm.

Bennett here develops the idea in Hoffmann's 'Suppen-Kaspar' of having characters gradually transform themselves into beasts symbolic of their vices.

*Struwwelhitler; a Nazi Story Book*. By Dr Schrecklichkeit [i.e. Robert and Philip Spence]. No publisher; no date. 176×140 mm. Peter Opie has written on the front endpaper of this copy: 'I bought this at the bookstall in Gloucester Road tube station when it came out in, I think, the summer of 1943, before I was interested in parodies of Struwwelpeter as such. We chuckled over it. Everybody who saw it chuckled over it. I still think it was one of the best parodies produced during the war.' P.O. 1955. 1st edition. Later printings have thinner paper cover and the imprint 'Published by The Daily Sketch and Sunday Graphic Ltd', at foot of p. 1.

*Struwelpeter* [sic]. London: David Bogue, n.d. [1855] (Funny Books for Boys and Girls). 212×166 mm.

Essentially Hoffmann's book, but with text and illustrations considerably adapted. A duplicate copy in the Collection has the title *Troublesome Children*.

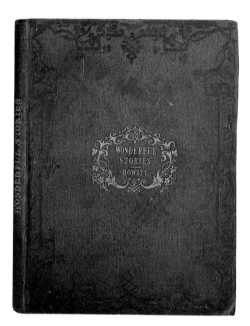

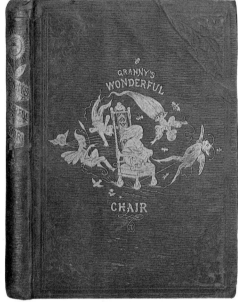

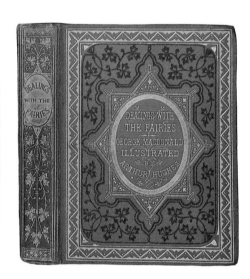

The Flowering of Fantasy.

*Wonderful Stories for Children.* By Hans Christian Anderson [sic], translated from the Danish by Mary Howitt. London: Chapman and Hall, 1846. 166×122 mm.

*Granny's Wonderful Chair and its Tales of Fairy Times.* By Frances Browne. With illustrations by Kenny Meadows. London: Griffith & Farran, 1857. 165×115 mm.

*Dealings With the Fairies* . . . By George MacDonald. London: Alexander Strahan, 1867. 135×102 mm.

Three early Victorian collections of fantasy-tales, rarely seen in such nice condition as this. (When the Opies acquired *Granny's Wonderful Chair*, the library at the British Museum possessed no nineteenth-century edition at all.)

*The May-Blossom*, from original illustrations by H. H. Emmerson. With verses by Marion W. Wingrave. London: Frederick Warne & Co., n.d. [c. 1882]. 252×195 mm.

*The Railway Children*, by E. Nesbit, with drawings by C. E. Brock. London: Wells Gardner, Darton & Co. Ltd, 1906. 202×138 mm.

Two early examples of publishers using pictorial paper covers to protect a book's binding. The glazed paper boards of *The May-Blossom* and the cloth gilt of *The Railway Children* have clearly benefited.

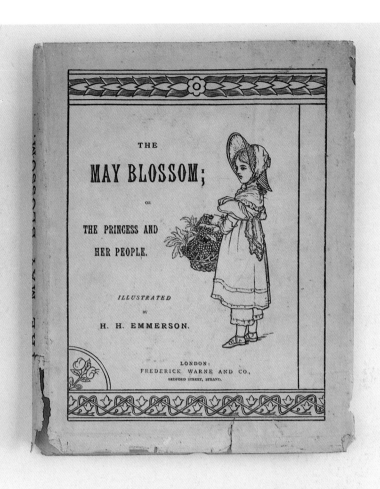

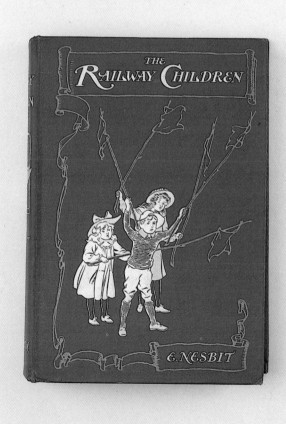

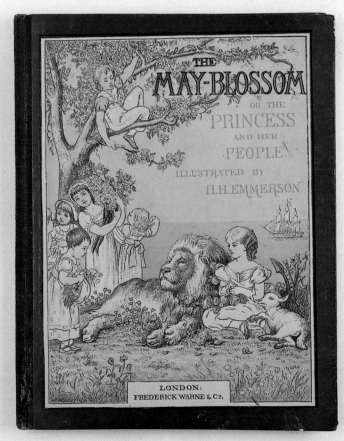

*The Tragic and yet Strictly Moral*
*Story of how Three Little Pigs Went to Market and the Old*
*One Stayed at Home.* Related in
eggs-hameter, illustrated with cuts from Bacon, and printed
in pigment. London and Edinburgh:
G. Waterston & Sons & Stewart, n.d. [*c.*1880]

The title, which typifies
Victorian punniness, conceals a drastic story in which Mother
Pig cooks and eats her children in
mistake for pancakes and then expires from the medicine that is
prescribed for her. What is also of
interest, however, is that this relatively obscure
Scottish toybook is illustrated by
Charles Doyle: brother of the great *Punch* illustrator,
Richard, and father of the creator of Sherlock Holmes.

*Park's Amusing History of Simple Simon.*
London: printed by A. Park, n.d. [*c.*1850]. 170×108 mm.

*The Story of Simple Simon*; illustrated by Frank Adams London
& Glasgow: Blackie & Co. n.d. [*c.*1908]. 285×225 mm.

*Simple Simon*; illustrated by Frank Adams. London & Glasgow:
Blackie & Co., n.d. [*c.*1938]. 254×195 mm.

Variety and longevity in a nursery-rhyme picture book. Park's
prettily hand-coloured edition was
based on a cruder original. Over thirty years Frank Adams's
version also varied.

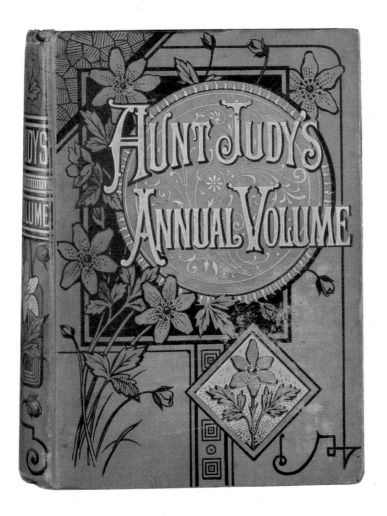

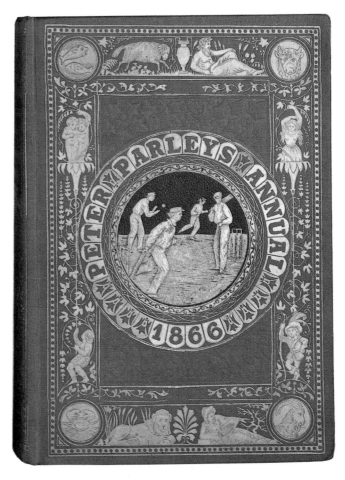

Six examples of nineteenth-century
children's magazines, bound up as presentation annuals:

*Aunt Judy's Annual Volume.*
Edited by H. K. F. Gatty. London: Bemrose & Sons. 1884.
195×135 mm.

Although this volume lacks its
Caldecott frontispiece, that is made up for by the inscription:
'Alfred Gatty from his loving daughter
H. K. F. Gatty Oct 1884'.

*Peter Parley's Annual* for *1866.* London:
William Kent, 1866. 195×135 mm.

Includes an almanac and a diary, improving articles,
and a final 'Commercial Addendum' with
advertisements and notes on various manufacturers.

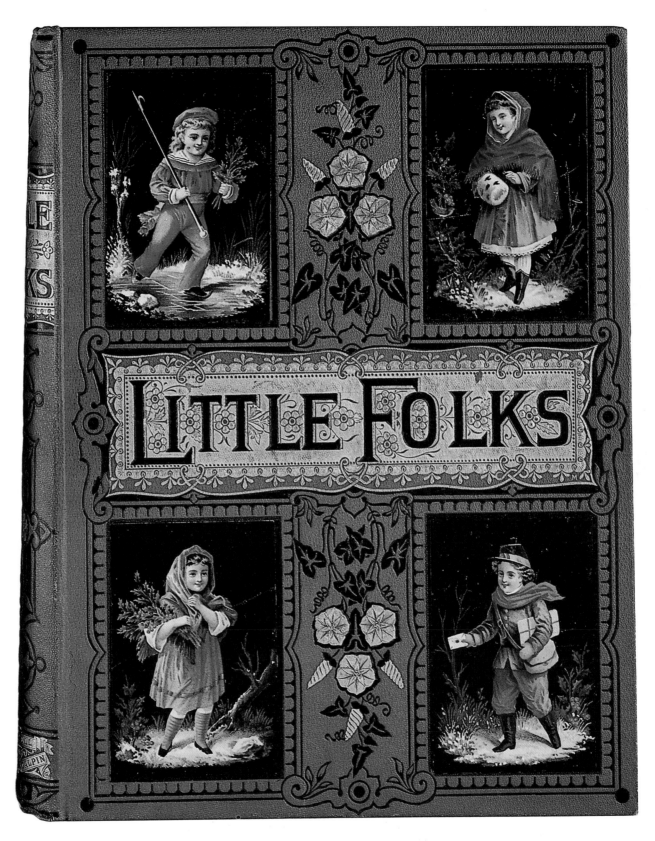

*Little Folks. A magazine for the young.* London: Cassell, Petter
& Galpin, n.d. [for Christmas 1877]. 235×180 mm.

A binding-up of Parts 129–152 to make a Christmas
compendium. This volume includes several illustrations by Kate
Greenaway.

*The Infants' Magazine.* Vol. XXIII. London: S.W. Partridge &
Co. 1888. 210×157 mm.

An improving magazine, with big pictures for young children.

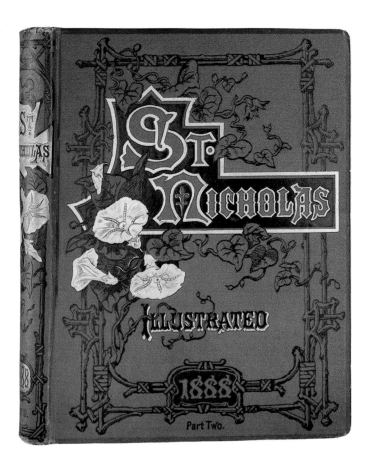
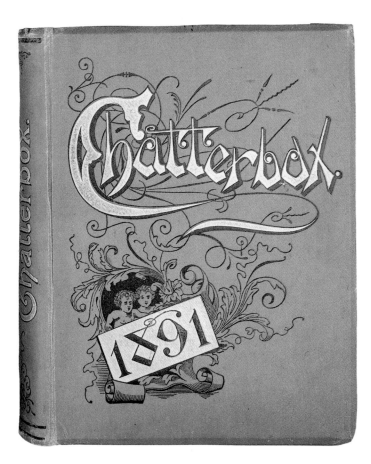

*St. Nicholas; an illustrated magazine for young folks.*
Conducted by Mary Mapes Dodge.
Vol. XV, Pt II., May–Oct 1888.
New York: The Century Co.; London: T. Fisher Unwin, 1888.
237×178 mm.

Among the contents is the serialization of T.N. Page's 'Two
Little Confederates' and the customary 'Brownie' drawings and
verses by Palmer Cox.

*Chatterbox.* Edited by J. Erskine Clarke, M.A.
London: Wells Gardner, Darton & Co., 1891. 240×180 mm.

Bound up weekly parts, with various lithographed colour plates.

A nostalgic glimpse for those who had 2d. – or 3d. – or even
4½d. to spend in 1954: a selection of the comics
that were to be found on the bookstalls during the week, of
September 25. Altogether the Opies bought about
thirty-six different comics that week, with some eight
story-papers and magazines.

Children were questioned on their likes and dislikes. Margaret
and Aprille declared that comics helped them with
their reading or 'to do better compositions'; Barbara liked them
because she didn't have time to read books; and
Peter had problems with his dad, who read them as well and
got annoyed when he couldn't find them.

# PART TWO

# TOYS AND GAMES

# INTRODUCTION

The child's toys and the old man's reasons
Are the fruits of the two seasons.

William Blake

**T**he Temple, where the toys are kept, is not intended as a place of entertainment for children; rather, it is a place where adults may meet their own childhood selves, or, through the powers of imagination, can reach out to the children of the more distant past who have loved these toys. 'Love' is not too strong a word. The love felt for a teddy bear or a Meccano set will endure for a lifetime, though for most of that lifetime they may be parcelled away in a cupboard. Such love has no relation to the size or expensiveness of the toy. It is a response to its colour, smell, taste, shape and tactile quality; as well as to something about it that is infinitely endearing, and can possibly only be discerned by the owner. Even more it is engendered by possession (thus foreshadowing the possessiveness of sexual love). The Rev. Lord Sydney Godolphin Osborne, in a letter to *The Times* of 5 January 1865, feared that possession 'will beget selfishness', and believed that toys should be 'the property of a nursery commonwealth'. Never could a man have been more wrong. Why play with a communal teddy bear, who is so little attached that he will go to bed with *anyone*; and might indeed be so emotionally detached as to remove himself to some other family? Far better to risk the wrangles of *meum* and *tuum*, and to learn something of real life at its most fundamental.

Here in the Temple one can understand the attraction of some of the toys to their first owners. Handling a nineteenth-century thumb top, for instance, one approves the smooth feel of the boxwood and the tiny elegantly turned shape, as well as the astonishing movement of the top, which starts spinning on its head and rights itself on to its leg (a movement that can also be achieved by spinning a drawing pin, though less aesthetically). And the particular charm of the tin stag-beetle can be felt. A popular street toy of around 1900, its wavering legs, brightly painted wing-cases in assorted patterns, and erratic progress on four small wheels, make affectionate mock of all beetles everywhere. It probably cost ½*d*.

The principles on which the toy collection was assembled were these. To acquire chiefly the common toys that would be familiar to everyone, particularly those which were cheap and fragile and which, in most homes, would probably have been damaged and thrown away (toys such as a wind-up celluloid Japanese lady, and a cardboard helicopter – both *c*.1910). To represent the different kinds of toys with enough examples to show their development (though not their whole history), especially in regard to the materials used. Thus the game of knucklebones is illustrated by a knucklebone *in situ* in the skeleton leg of a sheep, a boxed set of real bones produced by J. Jaques & Son *c*.1900, and a boxed set of plastic bones as sold today in France. And the bird-call water warblers are found in various styles from timeless colour-glazed clay to early 1920s unpainted tin and to the refinements of modern plastic.

The wall of 396 cardboard boxes on the left of the Temple as one enters provides a rudimentary analysis of the smaller, cheaper toys, tricks and games. Thus a section entitled 'Schoolchild Humour' is divided into Buttonhole Squirts; Startlers; Vibrators; Jumpers; Spoofs Unpleasant; Spoofs Edible; Irritants; and Hand Shakers. And the only slightly more sophisticated humour of the office boys of the City of London (they who used to read the lurid adventure stories known as 'bloods' while dangling their legs over Waterloo Bridge) is represented by joke pencils with rubber points, pens that collapse or explode, drinking glasses that are impossible to drink from, and soap that washes black. Traditional toys have been given added meaning by being sorted under their motive power: hence 'Traditional Toys' mechanical; utilizing gravity; elastic powered; wind operated; with lever movement; circumgyratory; and string operated.

Peter Opie so treasured the small, cheap, and, he felt, more evocative toys in the collection (toys from Christmas stockings, or from a schoolboy's pocket) that sometimes the more imposing toys seemed to be there only on sufferance. Yet even as the progenitors of the common toys they have their place. The Queen Anne doll had to come before the ordinary Dutch dolls; the 1766 dissected map before the cheap cardboard jigsaw puzzles; the elegant Regency box of Changeable Ladies before the mass produced booklets of heads-bodies-and-tails. They, and the other key playthings such as the dolls' house, the rocking horse, the early child's bicycle, the Leotard sand toy, the zoetrope and praxinoscope, might indeed be considered the aristocracy of the nursery.

A wooden cylinder box containing cardboard discs printed with pictorial letters of the alphabet. This is thought to be the first 'object' to arrive in the Opie Collection. Although clearly related to children's reading it marks a move towards the collecting of toys and games as well as books.

# BABY AND TODDLER

Small traveler from an unseen shore,
By mortal eye ne'er seen before,
To you, good-morrow.

Cosmo Monkhouse, 'To a New-Born Child'

Parenthood would be less expensive if babies were left to entertain themselves as the offspring of other mammals do, by playing with their own fingers, mouths, ears and toes, by listening to their mother's wordless crooning and pulling at her hair, and, as they grow stronger, by rough-and-tumbling with their siblings.

But human beings, restless and inventive, have elaborated all these instinctive activities. Toys are now grasped by the exploring fingers, acting as intermediaries between the baby's own self and the world outside. Words and tunes have supplanted the wordless crooning, and the words and tunes have been printed in books. The rough-and-tumble games have acquired rules.

This elaboration (the process of culture) has given the realm of childhood ingenious toys which entrance children and adults alike, nonsense songs and haunting lullabies, and structured games which have become the passion of nations. It has also given us the concept of bestowing upon children, at the outset of their lives, gifts which will bring them happiness and success.

The earliest gifts to the newly born were not for the baby's use at all, but were inaugural and symbolic. The Three Wise Men brought to the Christ Child gold which signified His royalty, frankincense in token of His divinity, and myrrh foretelling His agony and death. Ordinary babies, in later centuries, were presented with three magical gifts on the occasion of their first visit to a neighbour's house, the gifts usually being an egg representing fertility, and a silver coin and some salt for protection against evil. The benign power of silver can be seen, too, in apparently practical gifts such as christening mugs and silver rattles.

A silver rattle of *c.*1830, with the customary whistle, bells and coral stick. Often given as christening presents, rattles like this were both an entertainment and a teething stick for the baby. The rattle also has magical properties: red coral has been powerfully protective since classical days, and bells have been used to drive away evil since earliest recorded history.

Having given the child a propitious start, the adult world begins to equip him with the paraphernalia which has been found, over many generations, to make babies nicer to live with, and to incline them towards civilisation. Movement is known to entertain the very young, and when parents are exhausted with giving knee rides, aerial tossings, piggy backs and twizzlers, the burden of locomotion can be transferred to a rocking horse or galloping gig. Interesting sounds, textures and colours are provided by means of rattles, squeaky toys and mobiles, for stimulation or diversion. Indestructible books appear, which are scarcely more than intriguing objects to be flapped over page by page in the pram, and yet are full of pictures which must be

One of a range of glamorous plastic rattles produced by an unnamed Far Eastern country in the early 1960s. This example was bought in Woolworths in 1961, and cost 6d. Within the mermaid's rotating fish-tank are a lobster, a fish, a sea-horse, a starfish, and some tiny plastic pebbles which rattle when the wheel is spun round.

Pincushions like this were made by devoted friends and relations to await the coming of the 'little stranger'. They were adorned with floral patterns of new pins, enclosing messages carefully devised to be suitable for either sex, such as 'Welcome as the Summer Flowers' (above) or 'Father's hope and mother's joy, Welcome either girl or boy'. Their underlying symbolism was, however, stronger than any welcoming message. Cushions have a significance of their own (*vide* the ceremonial presentation of the Coronation Crown, and of Cinderella's glass slipper); and pins, especially new pins, are an ancient defence against witchcraft.

matched with words and rhymes – pictures and words which have to be taken on trust, sometimes ('A is for Aard-vaark') by the presiding adult as well as the child.

A friendly relationship with the letters of the alphabet can be established in childhood which will last a whole lifetime, and the wily parent introduces them in all manner of pleasant contexts: as sweets and biscuits; on the child's mug and plate; and as separate letters of wood, ivory, or plastic which can be played with as did Cowper's 'unletter'd boy, Sorting and puzzling with a deal of glee, Those seeds of science called the ABC'. (It is sad that numbers are less often turned into playthings, and that the fat and comfortable B is thus better loved than the equally comfortable 8.) The height of captivation is reached when the alphabet is combined with several other delights, for instance when animals (a child's natural allies and friends) are depicted with their initial letters on those hollow building bricks which can be piled on top of each other and, when the time comes for clearing the nursery floor, can be nested inside each other like a Chinese puzzle, thus justifying Nanny's absurd dictum that it is 'as much fun putting the toys away as it is getting them out'.

A squeaky book of the 1920s. The verse reads:

Press my tiny hand – and hear Me call aloud for Mammy dear

The hand-coloured key-block for the nursery scene in Caldecott's *Hey Diddle Diddle and Bye Baby Bunting*, 1882. The key-block was printed in sepia for Caldecott to colour, when he also put in much of the detail, such as the pattern on the mother's dress. The picture reflects the warmth and cosiness of a nursery of those days. Baby Bunting is held safely on her mother's knee, while the nurse airs her clothes on the fender before the nursery fire and her brother acts out the hunting scene astride his hobby-horse.

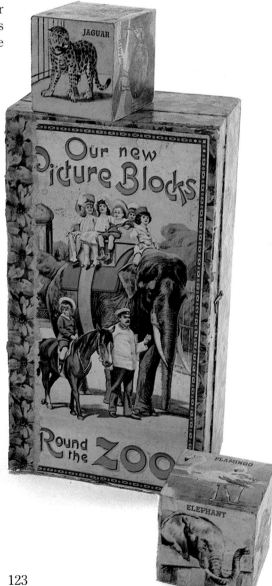

'Our new Picture Blocks – Round the Zoo'. These are of course blocks decorated with complete pictures, as opposed to the blocks bearing part of a design which must be put together like a jigsaw puzzle to make a complete picture (see page 152). They are the kind of blocks that adults balance on top of each other for a baby to knock down, the baby then graduating to being the builder. They can also introduce a toddler who has never been to a zoo to the exotic animals who live there. The boys on the pictorial label are wearing 'shorts', the new short trousers which came into fashion in about 1895, so probably the blocks were made at about the turn of the century.

This rocking-horse is called 'Spink's Folly'. The firm of Spink and Son, medallists to Her Majesty the Queen, bought it 'to amuse the staff', they said, at Christmas, 1966. On 28 December the horse appeared in a news item in *The Times*, and the Opies placed an order for it on Spink's answering machine, which was confirmed later in the day. Spink's, who are also picture experts, estimated the horse's age by the 'craquelure' or shrinking of the paint: 'We will guarantee,' they said, 'that it is more than 130 years old.' Unfortunately they had had it saddled in the modern manner by Parkers of St Martin's Lane, believing that 'some rich daddy' would buy it for his child.

A push-chair known as a 'galloping gig', equipped with two horses which move to and fro as the chair is pushed along. Push-chairs like this were made over several decades, and the style of the seat varies; but this particular model is exactly the same as that belonging to George VI at the age of one, in 1896.

Dean's Rag Book Co. was the first to print babies' books directly on to cloth (the pages of previous 'indestructible' books had been paper mounted on linen); and Dean's invented the term 'rag book', which is not recorded in the Oxford

English Dictionary before 1905. The earliest of the above group is *Rock a Bye* (bottom left), Patented 'U.S.A. Mar. 7 1905', which has a picture of a 1904 penny, but no series number. *Noah's Ark ABC* (top right) was No. 8 in the series, but is not dated. *Bo-Peep's Rhyme*

*Book* (bottom right) is the copy from the publisher's archive, as is *The House that Jack Built*, No. 148; they were published in 1912 and 1916 respectively. All of them bear Dean's rag book trade mark on the back, of two dogs having a tug-of-war with a Dean's Rag Book.

Mid-nineteenth-century alphabet books. Top: *The Nursery Alphabet*, Frederick Warne & Co., *c.*1870, No. 33 of Aunt Louisa's London Toy Books. Middle: *Green's Alphabetical Panorama*, Darton and Co., *c.*1860, in The Little Englishman's Library series. Bottom: *Mama's Little Pet's ABC*, one of 'Read & Co.'s Inimitable Toy Books'. *c.*1860.

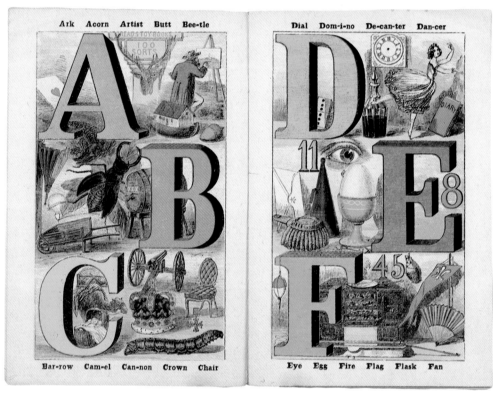

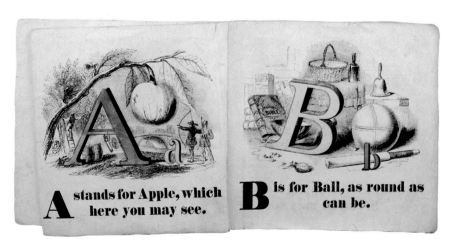

Twentieth-century alphabet books.
Top left: *Jolly Alphabets*, Blackie, *c.*1930.
Top right: an *ABC* typical of the cheap
publications of the 1960s. Bottom: *The Funny Bunny ABC*,
Thomas Nelson and Sons, n.d., *c.*1925.

# COMPANIONS

. . . for old sakes' sake she is still, dears,
The prettiest doll in the world.

Charles Kingsley, 'The Little Doll'

Antonia Fraser, in *A History of Toys*, wonders why the arrival of the baby doll was delayed until the nineteenth century; but babies are much less companionable than people of one's own age, or preferably a little older. As with the perpetually interesting question of why one strikes up a friendship with a particular person, the reason why a child is fonder of one doll than of another seems incapable of explanation, least of all by the child. Neither can sales figures be used as a guide to popularity, for a child can be given a 'Doll of the Year' who can speak whole sentences, and yet push it to the back of the toy cupboard and go on playing with the battered monstrosity she already knows.

Alice Meynell, in *Childhood*, says 'children . . . like homely toys, toys that can be clasped very close'. They are faithful to old friends, and grieve bitterly when a toy is lost; whatever the initial attraction may have been, it is long co-habitation that counts in the end, and the security of a real relationship. The small Letitia Penn took her wooden doll and namesake with her when her father William took his family out to the American colony about 1699, a reassuring companion on a long journey; John Betjeman rallied remarkably when his teddy bear Archibald was rushed to his hospital bedside after a heart attack. The Opie eighteenth-century doll lost her name many owners ago, and seems happier for having been given the title of 'Miss Notable'; but somehow one feels that the French clockwork doll is too self-sufficient, too much of an exhibitionist, to need a name or ever to have inspired much affection.

Old portraits of children show them hugging or playing with a pet animal more often than holding a doll. Now that squirrels, monkeys, parrots, pet lambs, and even kittens and lapdogs no longer live in such unfettered intimacy in the household, has their place been taken by the crowd of stuffed toy animals that accompany today's children – not just teddy bears, who are almost part of the family, but a large outer circle of penguins, owls, lions and tigers, snakes and tortoises?

Dolls, toy animals, and live pets arouse (especially in girls) feelings of parental concern as well as friendliness. A girl will naturally make jackets and trousers for her teddy bears, and provide them with home-made schoolbooks, and

Dutch dolls grouped round *The Golliwogg's 'Auto-go-cart'*, *c*.1901. According to the Colemans' *Collectors' Encyclopaedia of Dolls*, Dutch dolls were made in Grödner Tal, Austria (now in Italy) from the late eighteenth century, some being painted and finished in Bavaria, and probably also in Thuringia. They seem to be either the descendants (or, if collaterals, the poor relations) of the much more elaborate wooden dolls which were popular throughout the previous century, from at least as early as 1695 (see 'Miss Notable' on page 134). *The Golliwogg's 'Auto-go-cart'* was one of a series of much-loved books about a family of Dutch dolls and their friend the stalwart 'Golliwogg' (an invented character) by the artist Florence K. Upton, with verses by her mother Bertha Upton.

Deftly they help their pilot down
Then tear the rope away,
Weg stands on guard till all is safe
And none their flight shall stay.

Gliding along the grass they note
The watchman slumbering still,
And creeping slowly up the road
Soon cross the sheltering hill.

Cottager's doll. This Dr Doolittle-ish wooden figure represents the lower end of the doll hierarchy. He was brought into the West Liss antique shop by a local woman who said her grandfather had made him for her, when she was a child. His body and top hat are made from a single piece of pear-wood. His arms and legs are made of rope. His shirt is made from a scrap of pyjama material, and he wears a velveteen suit.

Pat, the youngest in Iona Opie's family of thirteen bears. In 1935, when Iona was twelve, the household drew a ticket in the Irish Sweep, and she and her sister were each allowed £10 to spend. Pat was sitting at the top of the staircase in Beales of Bournemouth, and it was love at first sight. He cost £1. He has always been the most outgoing of the family – probably because he was the only one to keep his fur. The shaped-book he is reading is *Teddy Bear*, published by Valentine & Sons in 1907. It begins: 'The largest family of bears in the world is formed by the Teddy Bears. A very happy-go-lucky lot they are: no wonder children like to play with them.' Teddy bears had then only been in existence for five years.

skates for the winter. She will harvest acorns for a velvet pig, and cook up the leftovers of the Bournemouth rock for a whole tableful of dolls; whereas a boy expects his Archie Andrews doll to tag along without provisions, and, presumably, expects Action Man to forage for himself. The chief appeal of paper dolls is that, mother-like, one can design and make additional clothes. The maternal instinct manifests itself very early. People say that Bonzo, the mongrel pup created by G. E. Studdy in 1912, was loved because he was ugly; it was really because his pink toe pads are so like a baby's toes, and made little girls feel protective.

The dolls in dolls' houses are more like acquaintances than close friends. They live in their own world, and yet have an irritating inability to manage their own domestic affairs. The child who owns the dolls' house feels it is scarcely her responsibility. Mary MacCarthy remembers, in *A Nineteenth-Century Childhood*, her reluctance to do the tidying. 'There is the usual old worry to face of the wrong proportions of every thing inside the dolls' house that gives

me an uneasy feeling of helplessness; the heavy gold tea-set goes over at a touch, and sends all the chairs falling about, and knocks down the dolls – and there are other difficulties.' Useless for an older brother to suggest that it is all the fault of the male doll, who is a drunkard; the burden of responsibility cannot be shifted. Only adults should play with dolls' houses.

This toy lion is exactly as described in the Sears, Roebuck & Co. catalogue for 1912: 'Fur Covered Lion 95 Cents. Papier mâché lion in genuine calfskin cover, glass eyes, bushy mane and tail. Resembling a lion in every respect. Growling voice produced by pulling metal ring. Attached to wooden base on wheels. Length 11½ inches.' To be honest, the voice is more like the squeak of a piglet than the growl of a lion.

*Pracht-Anzüge Einer Jungen Dame*. A boxed set of a doll and her fashion costumes, made for the European market, *c*.1845, by G.W.F. The English description on the label reads 'Costumes of luxury of a joung [sic] Lady – a modern Manequin.' This toy presupposes that it was every little girl's ambition to grow up and wear glorious dresses, especially perhaps the wedding dress (bottom left) with its bunches of grapes symbolizing 'the fruitful vine', and this may well have been so. The dresses have paper backs making a kind of sleeve, and the doll was pushed into them from the bottom upwards.

Opposite: *Miss Dollie Daisie Dimple and her Trunk of Smart Clothes all to Take On and Off*, which Hinde's, of City Road, London EC, would send securely packed to any part of the British Isles for 1/6d. The trunk has lists of the contents pasted on to the inside of the lid, as was customary in those days. On the left is a list of clothes: 'Sept. 1887. Cream Lace Dress . . . with Cardinal Red flannel Petticoat . . . Oct. 16. Red Cloth Ulster & Felt Hat. May 1886. Fancy Walking Costume . . . New Patent Corsets.' On the right is a list of 'Presents Received': 'from Uncle Will, a music folio, from Auntie Sally, a poodle called Flossie', and so forth. In the space between these lists Messrs Hinde have taken the opportunity to advertise some of their other products: Hinde's Patent Wire Brush for the Hair; Ellen Terry Hair Pins; and Hinde's Hair Curling Pins.

*My Lady Betty and her Gowns*, Our Pets Dressing Series No. 1, Raphael Tuck & Sons, 1895. A saccharine doll and her wardrobe. Note the details, such as the Dorothy bag attached to the sash of the pansy-trimmed dress, and the 'enormous over-trimmed hats' remembered by Gwen Raverat with such horror, 'which were fixed to the armature of one's puffed-out hair by long and murderous pins'. No doubt it was fun to decide what a 'Lady Betty' would wear, for the aristocracy were, to the ordinary folk of the time, what film stars were to become in the 1920s.

This dolls' town house is built in the same Italianate style, with Ionic porticos, as the streets of identical houses built over acres of South Kensington after the Great Exhibition of 1851, when the surplus funds were used to develop the land south of the Park. The dolls' house originally belonged to Miss Green, a farmer's daughter who lived near Colchester. She gave it to her pupil Olive Cant, who gave it to her eldest daughter Anne Gargiulo, who lent it on permanent loan to her sister Iona Opie. The 'revived Regency' drawing-room furniture is of the style introduced by the American designer Duncan Phyfe (1768–1854); and the fireplace looks rather like Alice's in *Through the Looking Glass*, 1871, with the same large mirror, draped mantelpiece, and clock under a glass dome. Dolls who live in dolls' houses are not as companionable as other dolls. The dolls' house owner finds herself more in the position of a playwright, deciding the course of their lives: 'Now they're going to have tea', 'Now they're going to bed', 'Now – oh *bother* – I've got to do their spring-cleaning for them'.

Coloured wood-engraving by Kronheim and Co. from *The Life of a Doll*, No. 6 in Aunt Louisa's London Toy Books, 1866. Mamma is giving Fanny the doll which, she tells her, is 'not a common doll . . . she can open and shut her eyes, say something like Mamma and Papa, and walk across the room'.

Hand-coloured lithograph from *The Two Dolls*, edited by 'Mrs Dorothea Twaddle' and illustrated by 'Mrs Dolly Trott', 1846. Henry gives the doll, Polly, a 'drive' in his toy-wheelbarrow, which overturns – thus showing how unwise it is to entrust a doll to the care of a boy.

'Miss Notable', named after the irrepressible young lady in Swift's *Polite Conversation*, is one of the prettiest of eighteenth-century dolls, finely carved, and having the blown-glass eyes, cricket-bat back, centipede eyebrows, and low-placed cheek colour of her type and time (*c.*1740). She seems to have been intended to be a country girl, in her raspberry-patterned cotton gown; and, appropriately, she came from an antique shop in Broad Street, in the Hampshire market town of Alresford. The ultimate descendants of such wooden dolls were the ordinary Dutch (i.e. *Deutsche*) dolls shown on page 128).

Opposite: This clockwork Bru doll of the late 1880s could only be a Parisian, with her fashionable clothes, pearl ear-rings, and confident stare. As she drives along she whips her horses and turns her head from side to side, and the horses move up and down.

# PLAYING AT LIVING

. . . sometimes for an hour or so
I watched my leaden soldiers go
With different uniforms and drills
Among the bed-clothes, through the hills;

And sometimes sent my ships in fleets
All up and down among the sheets;
Or brought my trees and houses out,
And planted cities all about.

Robert Louis Stevenson, 'The Land of Counterpane'

The best place to play at living is outside, making houses and forts from piled-up pine needles, floating sticks down streams, shooting bamboo arrows from hazel-branch bows, and making meals of dead-leaf toast and buttercup-petal butter, eaten off a broken tile. The

second-best place is peacefully in bed, while being ill. Grown-ups are usually sympathetic enough to provide a large tray to put across the bed, and on this can be emptied the family button collection to be sorted into sizes and colours and set up as theatres with actors and audience, or as chemists' shops, or schools, or restaurants with plates and dishes bearing different kinds of food and drink. The third-best place, although it is subject to passing adults and demands for clearance, is the floor.

It is a truism that when children play at living

'Flat figure' toy soldiers. Above and Below: part of a set depicting the Battle of Waterloo, and presumably made for the German and English but not the French market. In front of these, some English soldiers in their original chip box; the label of this 'No. 4' set of 'Engländer, Engl. soldiers, Anglais' shows that they were of German make for the whole European market.

with wooden bricks, model soldiers, toy cars, ships, farms, and railways spread out on the floor, their pleasure comes from creating a world entirely their own and under their control. They decide what goes where, and what happens when. They make the geography and the scenery from corrugated paper, cardboard, papier mâché, silver paper, cushions, and the less prestigious books. If, as is usually the case, their world resembles the real world, they pretend they are organizing real events and making real decisions: they take families in

*Deutscher Baukasten.* A box of building bricks, or 'architectural amusement', of *c.*1820. The bricks and turned columns are beautifully finished and smooth to handle.

trains for holidays on farms in the country; they crash cars and arrange for the occupants to be taken to hospital; they pitch camp, and line up opposing armies to shoot at each other with matchstick-firing cannon; they build houses and bridges and decide to knock them down.

When adults play with imaginary countries on the floor, as happened in the years of innocence before the First World War, they abandon the real world; they construct far-away islands and cities with temples and palaces, and have fantastic adventures. E. Nesbit wrote about such games in *The Magic City* (1910). H. G. Wells described them in *The New Machiavelli* (1911), *Floor Games* (1911) and *Little Wars* (1913); his countries were always at war with each other, and he thought that the games, as well as 'keeping boys and girls happy for days together', would build up 'a framework of spacious and inspiring ideas in them for after life'. 'The British Empire,' he said, 'will gain new strength from nursery floors.' Both authors played these games with their children; but with such forceful personalities in command one cannot suppose that the games were much fun for the children, and they may have been rather embarrassing.

There are other kinds of playing at living that are nearer the knuckle. To give a child a toy wheelbarrow or a Nuremberg kitchen seems an

An article in William Hone's *Table Book*, 1827, illustrated with an engraving, describes William Liston the war veteran who, having lost an arm and a leg, became famous as a street trader selling toy lambs. The article also recalls the maimed sailor who was credited with starting the toy-lamb trade some thirty-five years before, and whose musical cry was:

Young lambs to sell! young
    lambs to sell!
Two for a penny young lambs
    to sell!
If I'd as much money as I
    could tell,
I wouldn't cry young lambs to
    sell.

Liston's lambs were made by his wife and four children. They had 'white cotton wool for fleeces, spangled with Dutch gilt, the head of flour paste, red paint on the cheeks . . . horns of twisted shining tin . . . and pink tape tied round the neck'. The flock of lambs (below right) are in the same tradition, but their fleece is made from scraps of real sheepskin, and they are ornamented with rosettes of ribbon.

appalling form of coercion. Yet children will accept wheelbarrows, kitchens, carpentry sets and bus conductors' outfits, cooking stoves, toy Hoovers and fully-fitted doctors' bags without a qualm; and they leap delightedly into the roles offered them, only faltering when the toy saw is too blunt to be effective, the Hoover too feeble to pick up fluff, and the doctor's needle unable to puncture skin. The theory is, of course, that such toys give children a pleasurable attitude to work they will have to do when they grow older. It may be true.

Large black-painted tin cooking range, with copper pots and pans, kettle, and, in the centre, a boiler with tap to provide a constant supply of hot water. A cotton-padded tray to be saturated with methylated spirit, inserted in the central opening, and lit with a taper, meant that real cooking could be achieved.

**S**
Stands for STATION, with bustle and din,
Where some folks get out, and others get in.

**T**
For the TUNNEL, that's under the ground,
Here the whistle is heard with a very long sound.

**U V**
Stands for URCHIN, so simple and small,
Who cannot make out how the train goes at all.
V is for VIADUCT crossing the road,
Where the river beneath it is oft overflowed.

**W X**
Stands for the WHISTLE that often we hear,
When a tunnel is nigh, or a station is near.
X for the train that is called the X-PRESS,
That passes a mile in a minute, or less.

**Y**
Is YOURSELF, coming home
When lessons are all said

**Z**
Is the last of the letters we take,
Showing the ZIGZAGS the lines

EISENBAHN
RAILWA
CHEMIN

Foreground: a tin-plate French carpet train of *c.*1880, with locomotive, tender, two carriages, and a guard's van. The engine is named 'La Foudre' (Thunder), has a gilt boiler, and filigree hand rails; it can still pull the train across a carpet at a dignified pace. Centre top: a cheap boxed set made in Germany *c.*1890 for the Europe-wide market, as the tri-lingual label shows. The railway ABC book at top left is *Cousin Chatterbox's Railway Alphabet*, Dean and Son, *c.*1845; and on the right is *The Railway Alphabet* from the Aunt Mavor's Toy Books series, George Routledge & Sons, *c.*1880.

Coach, with coachman and
two wooden horses. It used
to stand outside the
Henderson dolls' house (see
Vivien Greene's *English
Dolls' Houses*, fig. 139) and
was presented to the Opie
toy collection by Mrs
Henderson's sister, Miss
Rogers-Tillstone.

Metal carriage, *c.*1870, with
two plaster people and a
disproportionately small
wooden horse. The people
have been provided with a
little floral mat to keep their
feet warm.

Tin horse-drawn tram,
advertising Colmans
Mustard, Pears' Soap, Frys
Cocoa, and Mellins Food.
Made in Germany. Late
nineteenth-century.

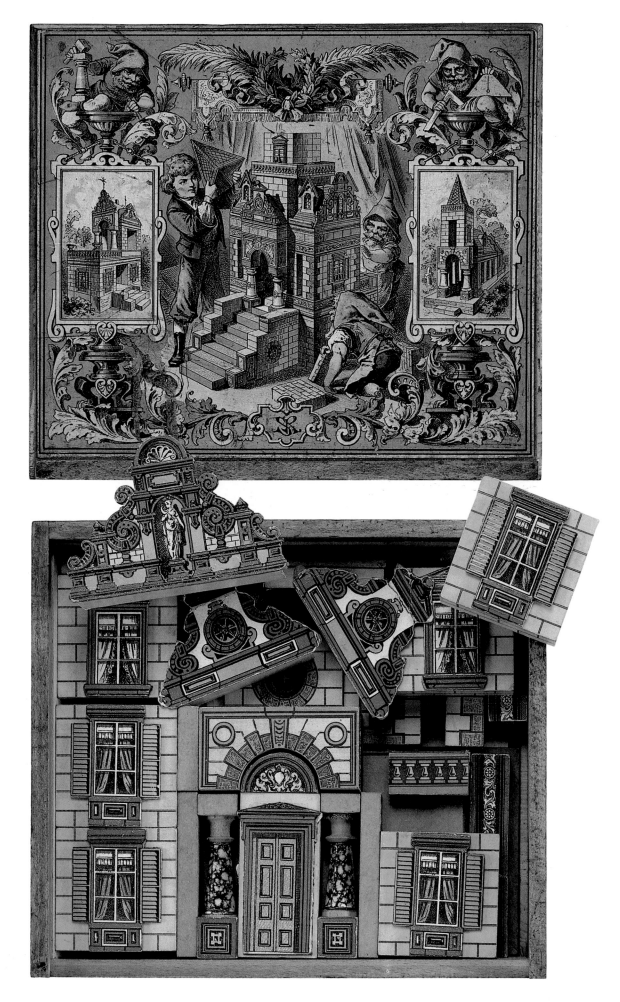

Triumph Building Blocks
c.1890. Triumph Building
Blocks justified their German
maker's claim, in six
languages, that 'No other
kind of Building-Blocks now
existing can show like
perfection'. The building
blocks are covered in paper
printed to represent bricks,
windows and doors,
palisades, ornamental
stonework and marbled
columns. Roofs and towers
are provided, and pasteboard
sheets which serve as floors
between storeys. The whole
building operation, as can be
seen on the lid, is under the
supervision of traditional
German gnomes.

# TOYS AND BOOKS THAT MOVE

When the Lord Jesus was seven years of age . . . he made figures
of birds and sparrows, which, when he commanded to fly, did fly,
and when he commanded to stand still, did stand still.

*Apocryphal New Testament*

Giving life is a god-like activity. A child may fervently believe that his or her toys live, and leave the toy-cupboard door ajar when she goes to bed so that the toys can come out to play during the night. But real divinity was attributed to the moving statues and talking heads of antiquity, which made oracular statements, and whose descendants were the automata – those wonderful mechanical figures and animals, made by jewellers and clockmakers for wealthy families, which reached their zenith in the eighteenth and nineteenth centuries.

Far better than winding clockwork and seeing a figure performing apparently of its own volition, are the direct satisfactions of the traditional toys, in which the power can be seen and understood, and the actions controlled. Consider the simplicity of powers such as these: the wind that turns the paper windmill on its stick, and wiggles the head and tail of the Nodding Turtle; the human puff that keeps the Magic Blow Ball suspended over the bowl of its pipe; the string that pulls the wooden crocodile along on wheels which, as the axles turn, move wires which open the crocodile's jaws and wag his tail; the lever movement that causes the monkey to make a somersault at the top of his stick; the

spring that makes the Jack-in-the-Box jump nearly out of his box; the knobs and rod that turn the Japanese god Daruma over on his horizontal bar; the weight inside the tilting round-bottom doll, which brings it quickly upright when it is pushed down; the mercury-weighted tubes that move the Chinese tumblers, of Regency days, over and over down their flight of steps; the gravity that pulls the twining snake down his stick; the string which moves the arms and legs of the Pantin clown up and down and the string which enables the little tin man politely to remove his hat; the ball on a string that,

An example of a traditional toy known in England as a Jumping Jack and in France as a Pantin. This pierrot 'pantin' is made of plywood and printed paper, and has real bells on his hands. A main string at his back pulls other subsidiary strings which make the arms and legs move up and down, a mechanism perhaps known best today from the popular contemporary carved Russian dancing bears.

Clockwork picture of Louis Wain-ish cats who jig up and down to a crisp rhythm, c.1870. The works of these German toys are unbelievably flimsy, consisting of a cheap clockwork mechanism, a string driving belt, and numerous pins and thin wire cogs. Like other childhood treasures, they are the descendants of toys made for adults, in this case the moving pictures made by clockmakers like Pinchbeck in the seventeenth and eighteenth centuries.

A little tin man who takes his hat off when the string is pulled, c.1910.

*Mov-I-Graff, c.*1910. When the card is vibrated the fine chain that forms most of the man's face moves to give him a different profile.

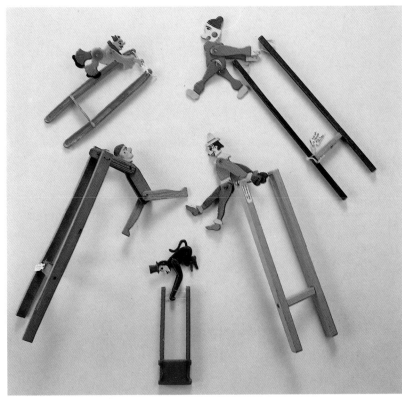

The acrobat who turns somersaults on twisted string must be one of the oldest and most ingenious of folk toys. When the pliable parallel bars are squeezed together at the bottom, the crossed string tautens and the acrobat is tipped over. Nineteenth-century examples of the toy are hard to find, so the Opies collected representative examples from the twentieth century. Top left: Fragile plastic acrobat made in Hong Kong. 6d in Woolworths, 1963. Top right: Cardboard acrobat on wooden bars. Made in Hong Kong, 6d, 1963. Middle left: Wooden. Bought in London street, early 1920s. Middle right: Wooden. Bought in Hamleys toy shop, Regent Street, London, 1954, for 1/6. Bottom: 'Plastic Monkey Acrobat.' Hong Kong. Bought at Barnums, London, 1961, for 5½d.

(forerunners of the manufactured books of heads-bodies-and-tails) in which two flaps are hinged to a page, one downwards from the top, the other upwards from the bottom, and of such a size that they meet neatly in the middle to form a picture. Home-made examples exist from the mid-seventeenth century. Peep-shows, in which a series of views are arranged at different distances to form a perspective, must surely have been made at home before they began to be produced commercially *c.*1825, for the raree-show had been a memorable treat at fairs since the seventeenth century. Thus the toy-book manufacturers tended to follow a tradition that already existed.

Perhaps the persistence of vision toys – the Phenakistoscope, Zoetrope and Praxinoscope Theatre – should be called not toys but wonders of science, for the cinema industry might be embarrassed at being dubbed simply 'the most successful of the toys that move'.

circling beneath the wooden platform on which a girl feeds her chickens, moves her arms up and down and makes the chickens peck; the sand that turns the wheel that turns Leotard's flying trapeze; the pliable hog's bristles on which the harpsichord figures are balanced, so that when the music is played the vibration swings their feet to and fro as they dance; the string that works the butter-cutter, which turns like a circular saw as the string twists and relaxes; the twisted string that forms the bar on which the acrobat turns his somersaults; the elastic which powered the 'Frog' aeroplanes of the 1920s, and which drives the Atomic Submarine (Hong Kong, 1965).

Paper toys that move, such as birds that open their beaks and Japanese cranes that flap their wings, have been around much longer than books that move. So have the turn-up booklets

Sand toy featuring Léotard, the man who invented the flying trapeze and, with his performance upon it (wearing a 'leotard', of course), was the sensation of London for a long season at the Alhambra music-hall in the 1860s. The motive power is supplied by a quantity of sand which is gathered into a hopper at the top of the box by turning it five or six times to the right; the sand then falls at random on to a wheel rather like a mill-wheel, and a spindle turns the bar of the trapeze, enabling Léotard to perform. A label on the box gives the maker's name: 'LEOTARD . . . Manufactured in mahogany case, and with Music, all sizes, and warranted for years, by Brown, Blondin, & Co.' (Have any survived 'with Music'?)

A Zoetrope (originally Daedelum) or Wheel of Life, with a selection of picture strips and base discs. The toy was invented by W. G. Horner of Bristol in 1834, but does not seem to have been put on the market until 1867. It works on the same principle as the Phenakistoscope (see page 146) but is a more sociable form of entertainment, since several people can look through the slots at once and see the individual pictures (as many on a strip as there are slots) apparently joining into continuous movement as the drum revolves.

Left: Praxinoscope Theatre, with detail from box (right) showing the apparatus in action. This was an elaboration of the Praxinoscope (from the Greek for 'action' and 'look at') invented by Emile Reynaud and patented in Paris in 1877, which was itself an improvement on the Zoetrope. In the Praxinoscope the slots of the Zoetrope are replaced by mirrors set round an inner drum to reflect the circling images; and in the Praxinoscope Theatre the reflections are viewed through a proscenium, and, for instance, a ballet dancer performs as if on a stage. When, in 1882, Reynaud projected similar moving pictures on to a screen before an assembled audience, the age of the cinema had virtually begun.

In 1823 Marc Isambard Brunel proposed and exhibited his plan for constructing a tunnel under the Thames from Rotherhithe to Wapping. It was a sensational project, and also a ready-made subject for a 'perspective'. Almost immediately the fancy stationers of Europe began to produce Thames Tunnel peepshows – thus greatly anticipating reality, for the tunnel was not finally opened until 1843.

The example above, published by 'M.B.' with French and German labels, is more elaborate than most, showing as it does the quayside, and traffic on the river, as well as the vaulted tunnel beneath, with its roadways and pavements for horse-drawn carriages and pedestrians.

A great variety of peep-shows were manufactured throughout the nineteenth century, perhaps the most famous being those made as souvenirs for the Great Exhibition, 1851; and the tradition did not quite die out, for a peep-show was on sale at the time of the Coronation, in 1953.

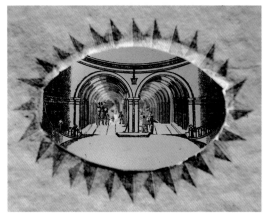

The Phenakistoscope illustrates the close connection between science and the world of toys. It arose from the work on optics being carried out by Dr Roget and Michael Faraday, and was the successor to the simple toy that first demonstrated the principle of persistence of vision – the Thaumatrope of 1827. The Phenakistoscope was invented (and named, using the Greek elements 'cheat' and 'look at') by Professor J. A. F. Plateau of Brussels, in 1832. Almost simultaneously, and quite independently, Professor S. Stampfer of Vienna invented a similar toy, which he called the Stroboscope (from Greek 'whirling round' and 'look at'). The arrival of moving pictures was no small event, and by the following year the leading print-makers of London's West End, and other unnamed firms at less prestigious addresses, were turning out sets of discs in large numbers, naming them *Magic Disk*, *Optical Illusions or Magic Panorama*, *Fantascope*, *Wheel of Wonders*, and so forth. Individual discs could display a touch of wit, as in 'Law and Equity' (centre back, above), which shows a man forking a lawyer into his mouth; or a flight of fancy, as in 'Journeying to the Moon' (immediately below previous).

The discs are about 24 cm across, with figures arranged radially upon them, representing moving objects in successive positions. A disc is mounted on the handle provided, and the viewer, standing in front of a looking-glass like the lady on the box lid (above), spins the disc round and sees, through the slots on the edge of the disc, the reflections of the figures apparently moving in continuous motion.

Above: Picture of a young lady painted on talc, with some of the set of twelve costumes which fit exactly over the portrait so that she can appear to be wearing a smart frogged coat and feathered hat, or a Turkish costume, or a Tudor costume, or even (far right) to have been changed into a young man. Second half of the eighteenth century.
Right: Two of twelve cards in a patterned slip case, which depict the sometimes flamboyant headgear of c.1815, with a lady's head which can be moved from one to another.

'Changeable Ladies', published by Ackermann, 1819. Each head is composed of three parts, and each part interchanges with the corresponding part in any other head, so that nearly five thousand different portraits may be formed. There was a companion set of 'Changeable Gentlemen'.

Opposite above: *Surprising Comical Characters . . . Capable of over five hundred Metamorphoses*, Dean & Son, c.1890. A heads-bodies-and-tails book in which the metamorphoses are part of a story.

Opposite: Walter Trier's *Crazy People*, c.1945. Trier was the Czechoslovak artist who, from its inception in July 1937, made the covers of *Lilliput* magazine so memorable.

    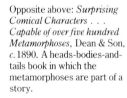 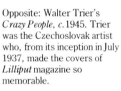

'Swoppets – Models that Swivel and Swop' were produced by Herald Miniatures Ltd in 1958, and were a sensation when they first appeared. The three figures on the cardboard mount (centre) cost 3/11d. Innovations in the toy industry are usually the result of 'cross pollination' between two established ideas. The heads, scarves, pistols, holsters, etc. which can be swopped between 'Swoppets' figures seem to owe much to the principle of the heads-bodies-and-tails toy books.

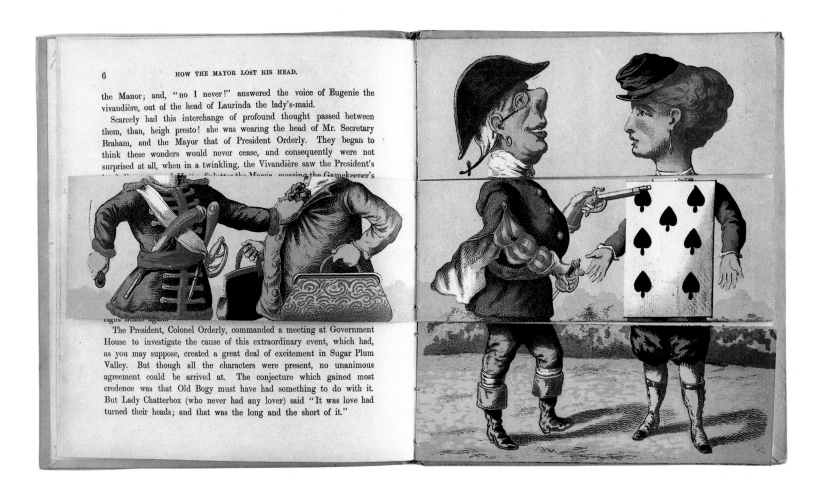

the Manor; and, "no I never!" answered the voice of Eugenie the vivandière, out of the head of Laurinda the lady's-maid.

Scarcely had this interchange of profound thought passed between them, than, heigh presto! she was wearing the head of Mr. Secretary Braham, and the Mayor that of President Orderly. They began to think these wonders would never cease, and consequently were not surprised at all, when in a twinkling, the Vivandière saw the President's

The President, Colonel Orderly, commanded a meeting at Government House to investigate the cause of this extraordinary event, which had, as you may suppose, created a great deal of excitement in Sugar Plum Valley. But though all the characters were present, no unanimous agreement could be arrived at. The conjecture which gained most credence was that Old Bogy must have had something to do with it. But Lady Chatterbox (who never had any lover) said "It was love had turned their heads; and that was the long and the short of it."

A child's 'boneshaker' bicycle of *c.*1870. It has wooden wheels rimmed with gutta-percha. Its pedals are fixed to the front wheel, so that when going fast downhill the feet must be held up in the air. An ingenious brake is brought to bear on the back wheel when a string, connected to the handlebars, is tightened by twisting the handlebars backwards towards the rider.

Raleigh Chopper bicycle, 1971. It was every child's ambition to own a Chopper in the early 1970s. The super-new design, with the rear wheel larger than the front, Sturmey-Archer 3-speed gear, and, especially, the 'Easy Rider' handlebars, meant that it had the prestige of a pedal-driven motorcycle and was capable of astounding trick performances, such as standing up on its rear wheel.

# CAN YOU DO?

Skill to do comes of doing.

Ralph Waldo Emerson, *Society and Solitude*

Co-ordination of mind, eye and hand characterizes these games. They are also competitive, even if the competition is against one's own last score, or against the obduracy of the toy itself. Most are international, and some are very old. Knucklebones and tops were known to the ancient Egyptians. Knucklebones, tops, marbles and yo-yos were played with in ancient Greece. Chinese puzzles of wood, wire and ivory, to disentangle and put together again, go back into unrecorded time; and some of the puzzles under glass seem to have an ancestry that connects them with the famous Maze of Troy Town. A cup-and-ball is shown in the margin of the manuscript *Romance of Alexander*, which was finished in 1344. The jigsaw and its congener the picture cubes depended on the advance of

emulation will not degenerate into envy. There is more danger that this hateful passion should be created in the minds of the young competitors, where it is supposed that some knack or mystery is to be learned before they can be played with success . . . We should show them that, in reality, there is no mystery in any thing, but that from certain causes certain effects will follow.'

Mystery there may not be, but these games require more technical skill than any others in the nursery, and a child needs to be given a demonstration and a few tips by someone who has played them in his youth. Failing an experienced adult, one of the bumper Victorian games books is a great help.

The Victorians were fascinated by engineering techniques and simple scientific experiments in a way that we seem to have outgrown (being, perhaps, afraid of appearing amateurish), and

printing, and were by-products of the increasing flood of maps and popular prints in the eighteenth century. The hit-a-pin bagatelle boards, though not known in this precise form before Regency days, are related to the game of billiards, played since the sixteenth century.

In the Edgeworths' *Practical Education* (1798), 'Toys which afford trials of dexterity and activity, such as tops, kites, hoops, balls, battledores and shuttlecocks, ninepins, and cup and ball' are commended as engaging children's senses, understanding and also passions. 'They emulate each other; but, as some will probably excel at one game, and some at another, this

*Europe, Divided into its Kingdoms &c.*, 1766. By J. Spilsbury. John Spilsbury was a London engraver and map-maker. By mounting his maps on thin mahogany board, and cutting them into pieces round the borders of the kingdoms or counties, he invented, in the early 1760s,

'Dissected Maps, for Teaching Geography', of which this is the earliest surviving example. He thus began the long history of jigsaw puzzles, though the term 'jigsaw puzzle' did not come into use until after the invention of the jig saw, a mechanical fretsaw, *c*.1870.

they studied the principles that motivate toys with unaffected enthusiasm. *The Modern Playmate*, edited by the Rev. J. G. Wood in 1870, for example, gives directions for playing Cup and Ball, 'the Flying Cone' (diabolo), games with marbles, games with tops ('It is absolutely necessary to make a top spin, and to do that requires some little skill'), Cockamaroo (hit-a-pin bagatelle), Bandilore (yo-yo), and Spillikins. Advice on playing the age-old game of knuckle-bones could, however, not have been found in such a games book; nor when it was manufactured by Jaques & Son *c.*1900 were the instructions particularly enlightening. A child wanting to

know the whole long sequence of variations would have had to enquire of the guttersnipes of London and Manchester, as they sat on the paving-stones playing at 'Buck and Gobs' and 'Bobber and Kibs'.

Jigsaw puzzles are a challenge, and give rise to a quite unwarranted feeling of triumph when completed. They need (as do most of the games of skill) special qualities of character. The young Queen Victoria explained those qualities to Lord Melbourne when giving him a lesson in Cup and Ball: 'I do it with perfect steadiness, patience, perseverance and tranquillity, which is the only way to do anything.'

Marbles have a primeval fascination, partly because of their global shape (planets can be seen, reassuringly, as rather special marbles) and partly because of their tactile quality. Glass marbles, however, have the extra charm of their mysterious world within; and those with

elaborate whorls and spirals, or sometimes small figures, inside them were often just collected for their beauty rather than being risked in a game, for they shatter very easily.

The old hand-made marbles pictured above were made from rods of clear and

coloured glass which had been pulled out (in the manner of seaside rock) to a length of 6½ feet. Marble-sized pieces were cut off the rod by means of marble scissors (invented in 1846), and the pieces were rotated in a wooden barrel to attain their fully-rounded shape.

When the marble scissors did their cutting, a rough place was left (the sign of a hand-made marble); and when the rod was twisted, in the final severing of the marble, the threads and ribbons of colour were brought together at the ends of the swirl.

*The Royal George, Or, Wooden Walls of Old England*, a dissected picture with its labelled box. *The Royal George*, pride of the English navy, sank at Portsmouth on 29 August 1782, while being refitted, with the loss of six hundred lives. This accident was a national catastrophe, and no ship was subsequently given her name. It seems inconceivable that a puzzle could have been titled 'Wooden Walls of Old England' *after* the sinking, so this must be one of the earliest known picture-dissections.

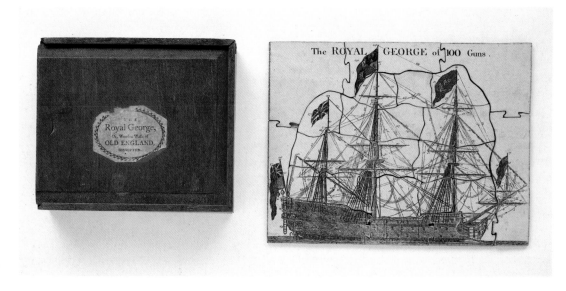

Left: *Johnny Gilpin Dissected, with the Story*. An example of print-makers' business methods in the late eighteenth century. John Wallis, of Ludgate Street, London, published a print of Cowper's 'John Gilpin' on 25 March 1785. On 1 October 1790 he issued it as a dissected picture, in a wooden box.

Opposite: Picture bricks made in Germany in the second half of the nineteenth century. The fact that they are bricks is less important than their ability, when put together correctly, to make one of six different pictures. The earlier set, at the top, has hand-coloured lithographs of rural German scenes. The later set (below) shows, on brightly printed glossy paper, dancing scenes from six countries, including (bottom centre) the Highlands of Scotland.

Yo-yo's. Some interesting variations on a world-wide folk toy which was known to the ancient Greeks. The three largest are probably survivors of the craze of 1789–90, when the toy was known as a 'quiz' in England and as a 'bandalore' in France. Thereafter, reading from left to right, are a Russell Super Yo-Yo, 'Made in Philippines', which advertises Coca-Cola; a 1971 Hong Kong yo-yo costing 5p; a 'Flying Disc' with a teddy bear inside, *c.*1960; a 1930s tin yo-yo advertising 'Force' Toasted Wheat Flakes, and below it a Japanese 'Return Top', 1966; a yo-yo advertising Libby's Milk, and bottom right, a Beginner's Yo-Yo of the classic Lumar brand.

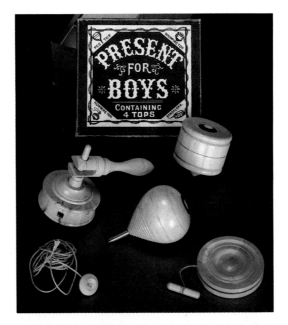

The pristine beauty of these boxwood and mother-of-pearl tops, in the state in which they might have been given to a boy on a Christmas morning a hundred and fifty years ago, can still arouse covetousness and pride of possession. The Opies tried to buy them from a young antique dealer at a fair in 1981, but he refused to part with them. 'I don't want to sell them *yet*,' he said. 'I loved them so much when I bought them, I took them to bed with me.' Peter had managed to negotiate the deal just before his death, so of course the surviving Opies carried it through.

The box contains a peg top, a whipping top, a humming top, and a bandalore (later to be known as a yo-yo).

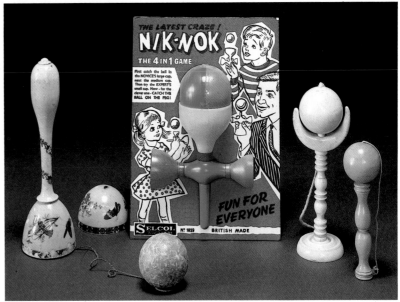

Cup-and-ball is the throwing up and catching game whose most famous exponents were Henri III of France (1574–89) and Jane Austen. The secret of success is given in the Rev. J. G. Wood's *Boy's Modern Playmate*, 1870: 'The learner should begin with catching the ball in the cup. He should take the stem by the middle. The ball should be thrown upwards by a slight jerk of the wrist, not of the whole arm; and, if properly done, it falls of its own accord into the cup. . . . The next feature is to *swing* the ball into the cup. . . . A good player should be able to catch the ball in the cup with his eyes shut. Now we come to catching the ball on the point. We have often caught it thirty times in succession.

With the fingers of the right hand give the ball a smart spin. Let it spin as far as it can in one direction and allow it to spin back again for ten or eleven times, watch that it is quite steady, and then throw it up as before. Turn the point upwards as if you were aiming at the spot where the string enters the ball and just as the ball touches the point let your hand sink slightly.'

Of the cup-and-ball games displayed above, one is painted with flowers; one is of ivory, and has a spike within a crescent on which the more skilful players may choose to lodge the ball; one is made of boxwood; and the fourth, of plastic, was launched by Selcol Products in 1966 as 'Nik-Nok – The Latest Craze!'

Wooden puzzles of *c.*1890. Some are named in Professor Hoffman's *Puzzles Old and New*, 1894. Back row: second from left, 'Barrel and Ball'; fourth from left, 'Fairy Tea-Table' cluster puzzle (top missing); fifth from left, 'Castle Money-Box'. Front row: left, the Aladdin Puzzle; second from left, a cluster puzzle called 'The Mystery'; third from left, 'New Persian Puzzle', and, just below, the beautifully turned, round box puzzle called 'The Wedding-ring Box'; far right, another cluster puzzle which Professor Hoffman names the 'Nut (or Six-piece) Puzzle', but which is usually called the 'Maltese Puzzle'. 'Cluster puzzles' have to be broken apart and put together again. The others are trick puzzles, of which the secret must be known, and the main principles involved are: (i) the puzzle unscrews in a place different from that expected, so that a coin or ring can be extracted; (ii) a peg is inserted to 'get a hold on the movable part' inside; (iii) a wire peg drops into a hole so that the puzzle can only be undone when upside down.

Opposite: Dan Dare bagatelle board, *c.*1955; and Regency 'chinoiserie' bagatelle board. Both are of the type that was called 'Hit-a-pin Bagatelle' during the 1930s craze. The balls are aimed at little numbered cups, and can be deflected by pins off which they bounce. The more evocative name in Regency days was 'The Rocks of Scilly'.

Most of these glass-topped puzzles were made in Germany *c.*1910, and in most the aim is to wiggle some small balls into certain positions in the pattern or picture. However, the First World War Zeppelin (bottom left) must be brought into the beam of the searchlight; and Bonzo, G. E. Studdy's popular dog character of the 1920s, must be given his bone. 'Squeak', in the centre puzzle, is from the famous 1920s comic strip 'Pip, Squeak and Wilfred' in the *Daily Mirror*.

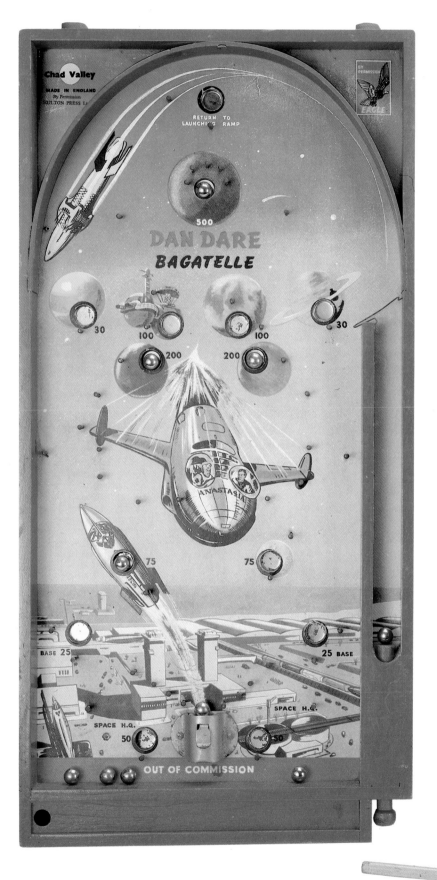

# SOCIABLE GAMES

The round game proceded right merrily . . . the whole table was
in a perpetual roar of merriment and laughter.

Charles Dickens, *Pickwick Papers*

Sociable games can be played at family gatherings by all the generations together, sitting round a table playing a race game, or flopped into a circle of armchairs after Christmas dinner playing a card game, with cards clutched closely to chests so that no one else can see. Or, more intimately, the games can be played by only two: a parent entertains a five-year-old kept home from school by a bad cold; or they while away the time together on a journey by train or aeroplane.

The presence of an adult or an older sibling is important to the conduct of a game when young children are playing, and prevents it from disintegrating into an uproar of accusations and denials of changing the rules, secreting cards, taking extra turns, giving the dice a flick when nobody was looking, or – the final get-out – upsetting the board on purpose. However, the right kind of adult will himself sometimes cheat, to the extent that, in games that have an element of skill, he will not play his hardest, thus giving his small opponent a share of success. For however much we reiterate 'It's only a game', or quote Kipling's advice about treating the triumph and disaster of 'those two imposters' just the

FORFEITS *Page 90*

same, children are not fools and they know full well that, as the old proverb says, 'He playeth best that wins.' They mind dreadfully if they do not reach the 'home' square of a race game first; and they feel a mortal shame if, in two unpleasant card games that have long been considered suitable for children, they end up as Donkey or (though not understanding the meaning of the epithet) Old Maid, and have to endure the customary jeering and the fingers pointed in scorn. It is only when the disciplines of gamesmanship have been learnt that children can, as young teenagers, graduate to games under their own jurisdiction; the card games of Pelmanism, and the deliriously exciting Racing Demon, for instance, which are best spread out on the floor.

Educationalists agree that taking part in group games is a necessary part of a child's life. In this way children learn the social virtues of restraint, and obedience to rules, of regard for others, and of being able to join in a general conviviality – for

Among the most popular indoor pastimes were the memory games in which a forfeit, which could be any small possession such as a thimble, had to be paid for every mistake, and redeemed when the game was over. The *modus operandi* of redeeming the forfeits is shown in the frontispiece to *Fireside Amusements*, by W. and R. Chambers, 1850 (left), which also describes 'a very difficult game of memory . . . the Gaping, Wide-Mouthed, Waddling Frog' (below left) published by Dean and Munday, in association with A. K. Newman & Co., *c.* 1822. In this game 'One of the players, handing anything he pleases to his neighbour, says "Take this!" The next answers, "What's this?" to which the first replies: "A gaping, wide-mouthed, waddling frog."
The second does the same thing to a third, adding: "Two pudding-ends would choke a dog; With a gaping, wide-mouthed &c.'
And so on through the whole party.'

The ritual of redeeming the forfeits (called 'selling pawns') is conducted thus: the mother (or the governess) takes charge of the pawns, and one of the children kneels with her head in the mother's lap, so as not to see whose forfeit is being redeemed. Mamma says, 'Here is a pretty thing, and a very pretty thing; what shall the owner do of this very pretty thing?' The seller asks, 'Is it fine, or superfine?' If it belongs to a boy, it is fine; if to a girl, it is superfine, and the punishment is awarded accordingly, 'giving of course the milder task to the fair sex'. The task could be saying 'five flattering things to the person sitting next [to] you without using the letter 'l', or kissing yourself in a looking-glass, or the puzzling undertaking of 'biting an inch off the poker', which is done by biting the air an inch away from the poker.

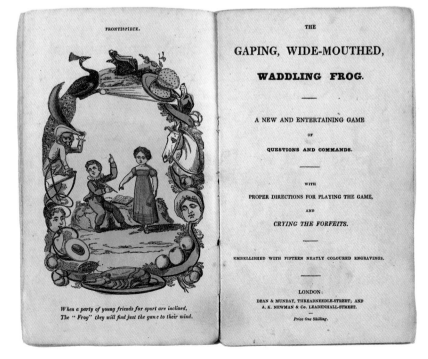

FRONTISPIECE.

THE

## GAPING, WIDE-MOUTHED,

### WADDLING FROG.

A NEW AND ENTERTAINING GAME

OF

QUESTIONS AND COMMANDS.

WITH

PROPER DIRECTIONS FOR PLAYING THE GAME,

AND

*CRYING THE FORFEITS.*

EMBELLISHED WITH FIFTEEN NEATLY COLOURED ENGRAVINGS.

LONDON:

DEAN & MUNDAY, THREADNEEDLE-STREET, AND
A. K. NEWMAN & Co. LEADENHALL-STREET.

*Price One Shilling.*

*When a party of young friends for sport are inclined,*
*The "Frog" they will find just the game to their mind.*

160

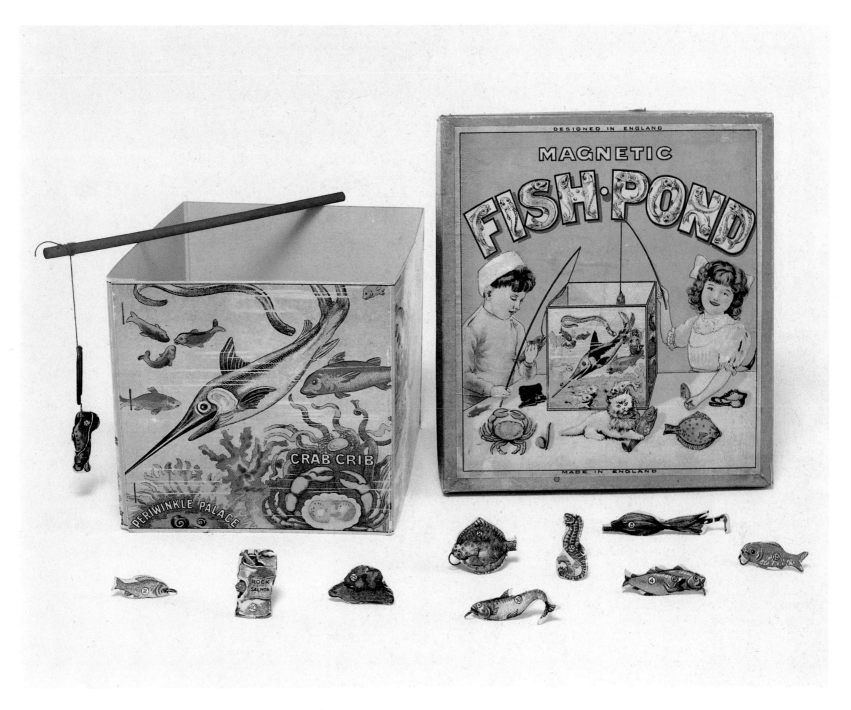

what would the social card and race games be without the exclamations of joy or dismay, the joking taunts and witty ripostes?

The production of children's race games, played with dice or teetotums, began in the eighteenth century. 'The improvement of youth' was in the forefront of the manufacturers' minds – the educational, not the psychological, improvement. They aimed to teach children schoolroom subjects in an entertaining way: history, geography, arithmetic, mythology and astronomy. They tried to instil an appreciation of the wonders of art and nature, and, through games of travel, to prepare the way for the

pleasures of the Grand Tour. They tackled morality head-on, with games such as 'A New Moral and Entertaining Game of The Reward of Merit', published by John Harris (1801), in which the players move through thirty-seven pictorial panels, each with a rhyme that points the moral. It begins with a picture of a lamb and a couplet giving permission to start the game ('As thou art harmless, never wild, Take up a Stake angelic child'), and ends with a picture of a schoolmaster giving the prize to the meritorious scholar. The more perspicacious children must have learnt, from such games, that chance plays a large part in one's success in life.

Magnetic Fish-Pond, *c.*1900. This game was very popular around the turn of the century, and has remained so to the present day. The fish have numbers printed on them, and metal rings in their mouths; the fishing lines are baited with small magnets. The charm of the game seems to lie in not knowing the value of the fish one has caught until it appears over the edge of the cardboard fish pond, or whether it might not be the old boot, which scores nothing at all.

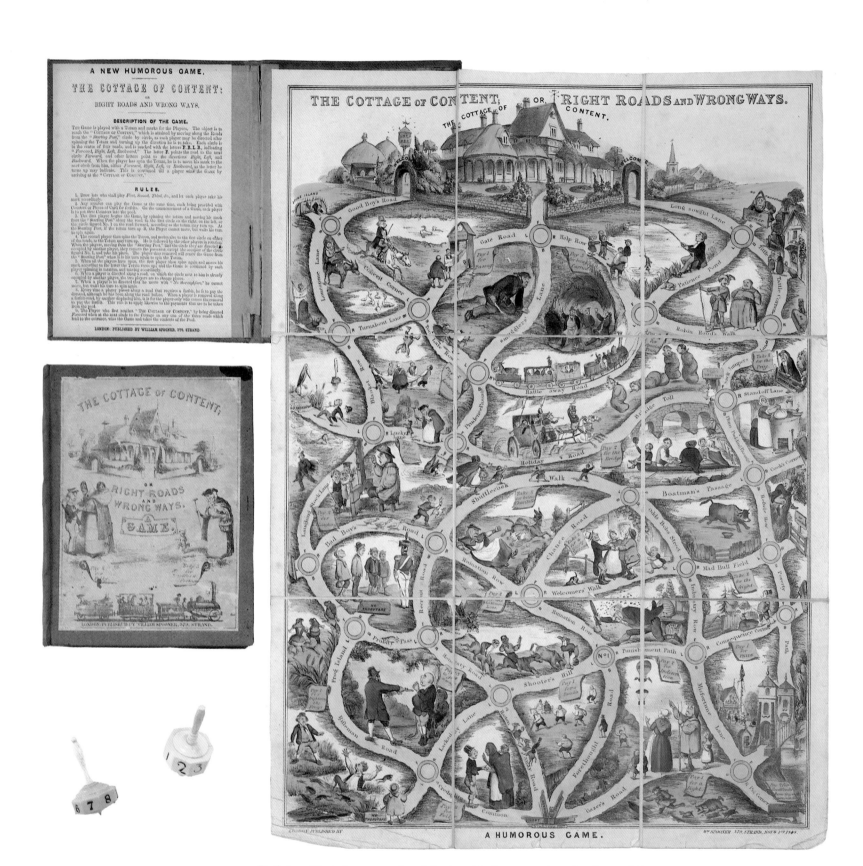

*The Cottage of Content; or Right Roads and Wrong Ways.* London: Published by William Spooner, 379, Strand. Nov.' 1st 1848, with its slipcase. In the mid-eighteenth century, race games began to be used for teaching purposes, the earliest being *A Journey through Europe, or The Play of Geography*, 1759, invented by John Jefferys. History, elementary mathematics, mythology and astronomy were also taught in this way; but children's race games designed simply for amusement were, in general, not produced until the 1830s, and even then they sought to instil some moral principles, as can be seen from *The Cottage of Content*. The players each had a marker or 'pillar', and a teetotum was used rather than dice, to avoid the risk (as one of the publishers said) of 'introducing a Dice Box into private families'.

*A Race through London, Interesting and Instructive for Young and Old, c.*1895. Printed in Bavaria. The label shows a scene of the 'Royal Exchange and Bank of England' with horse-drawn omnibuses and a hansom cab. (The 'Revotina' advertised on the left-hand bus is a hand-held patent musical box which was a craze at the time.) Six players could take part; and starting from Hampstead, Holloway, Stratford, Wandsworth, Dulwich, and Blackheath, each moved his little metal omnibus a total of fifty moves to reach the Bank of England in the centre.

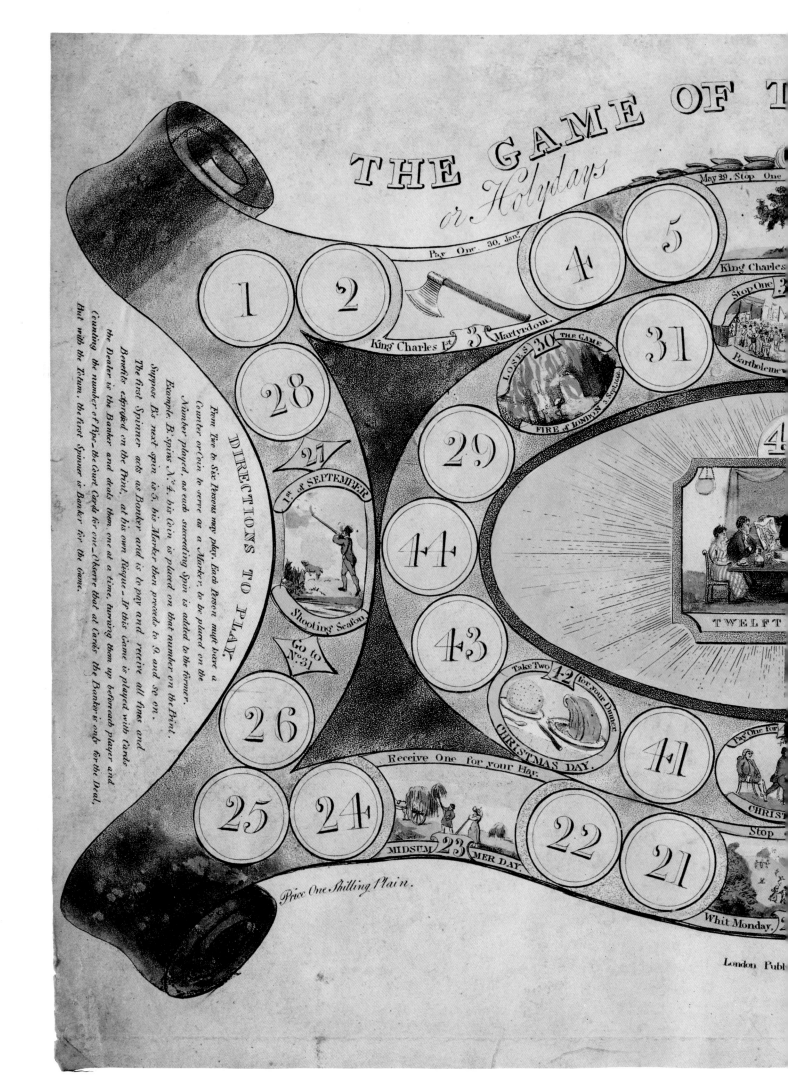

# THE GAME OF T[...]

## or Holydays

Price One Shilling Plain.

London Pub[...]

**DIRECTIONS TO PLAY.**

From Two to Six Persons may play. Each Person must have a Counter or Coin to serve as a Marker to be placed on the Number played, as each succeeding Spin is added to the former. Example B: spins N.º 4, his Coin is placed on that number on the Print. Suppose B's next spin is 5, his Marker then proceeds to 9, and so on. The first Spinner acts as Banker and is to pay and receive all fines and Benefits expressed on the Print, at his own Risque. If this Game is played with Cards the Dealer is the Banker and deals them, one at a time, turning them up before each player and Counting the number of Pips, the Court Cards for one. Observe that at Cards the Banker's ends for the Deal, but with the Totum, the first Spinner is Banker for the Game.

Pay One. 30. Jan.ʸ

King Charles I.ˢᵗ 3 Martyrdom.

1st of SEPTEMBER

Shooting Season.

Go to N.º 51

1

2

4

5

King Charles

Stop One 3[...]

Bartholomew

28

27

26

25

24

23 MIDSUMMER DAY.

Receive One for your Hay.

29

44

43

30 THE GAME LOSE.S. FIRE of LONDON 3 Septembr.

31

22

21

Whit Monday,

41

CHRISTMAS DAY.

Take Two 1.2 for your Dinner

TWELFT[...]

4[...]

Pay One for [...]

CHRIST[...]

Stop

May 29. Stop One

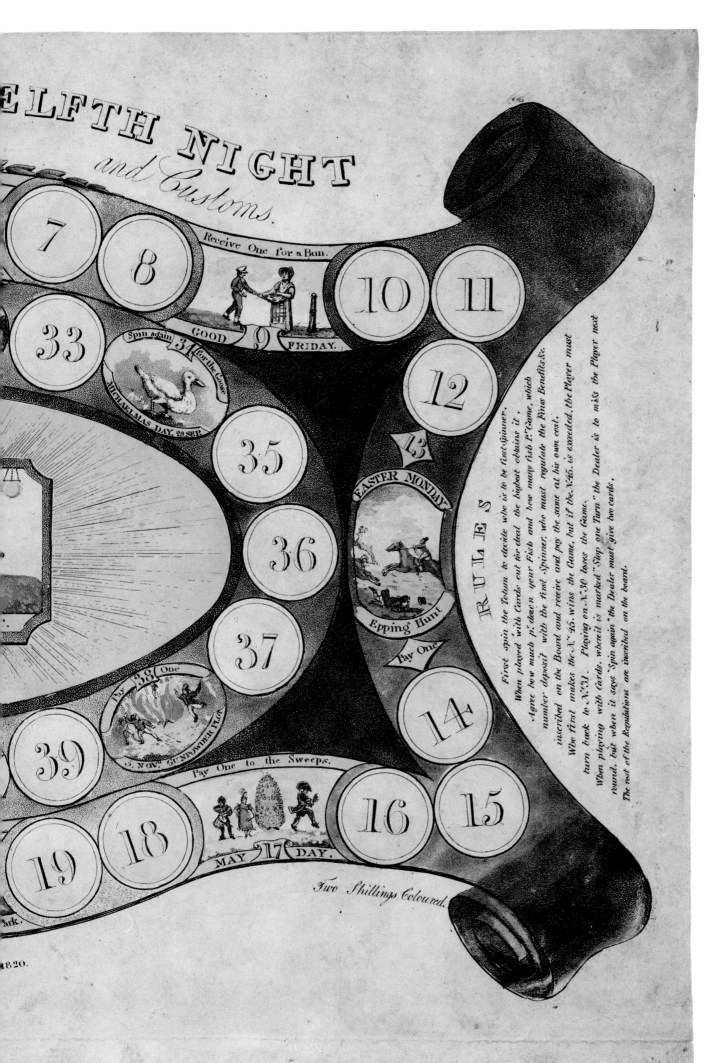

Children's playing cards of 1850–1910. The earliest and best known of these is Happy Families (top right). Sir John Tenniel drew the designs for it, and the publishers, John Jaques & Son Ltd, say the game was 'originally published before the Great Exhibition in 1851'. Another game which has entered the language is Animal Grab (top left), published by De la Rue & Co.: 'When a card is turned up having the same animal as one already exposed, either of the two players may make the cry of the animal depicted . . . and the one who does so first, takes the whole of his opponent's turned cards.' Top centre: playing cards based on the popular Dutch Doll books by Florence K. Upton.

WEG AND MEG.

Mrs. Grits the Grocer's Wife

Mr. Grits the Grocer.

Mr. Tape the Tailor.

Mrs. Tape the Tailor's Wife.

Mrs. Grits the Grocer's Wife.

the Grocer.

Tailor.

Tape the Tailor's Wife

Mr. Lion

Mr. Lion

"NOAH'S ...ARK" PICTORIAL CARD GAME

50

Containing Fifty-two Cards, from Original Designs.

COPYRIGHT.

LOADING THE DONKEY

A NEW ROUND GAME.

JOHN JAQUES & SON Lᵗᵈ

14 Find 'Twinkle, Twinkle!' said the Hatter

and the 'Dormouse in the Teapot'

AND THE CHESHIRE CAT.

6

8 Find the 'Knave' and the 'Lawyers'.

THE KING IN COURT.

GARDENERS TWO AND FIVE

6 Find 'Gardeners Two' and 'Five' and 'Gardener Seven'.

"OFF WITH THEIR HEADS" said the QUEEN

Board game confidently titled
'Halma' and decorated (punningly, one supposes) with pictures
of the battle of Alma, in the Crimean War.
The diagram is, however, that for the game of 'Fox and Geese'.

Opposite: *Game of the Star-spangled
Banner, or Emigrants to the United States of America*.
Published by J. Passmore, London,
*c*.1830. An aquatint map with numbers 1 to 147.

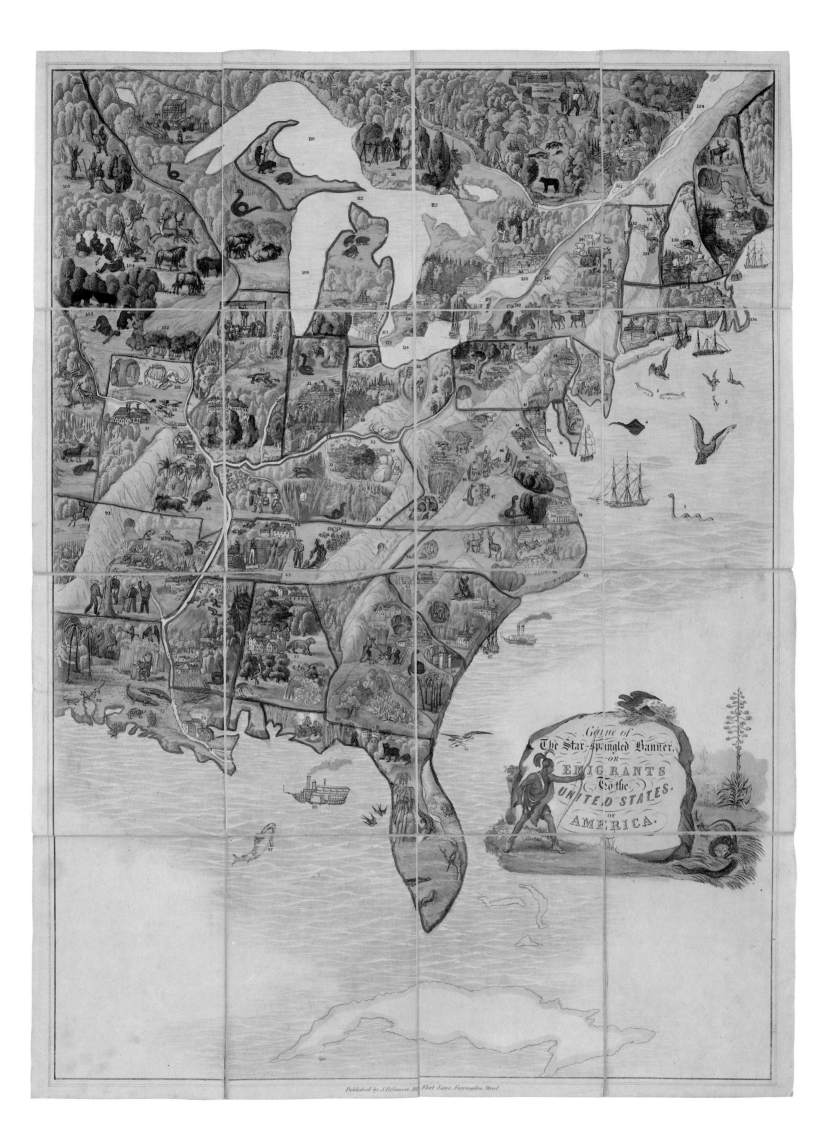

Game of
The Star-spangled Banner,
OR
EMIGRANTS
To the
UNITED STATES.
OF
AMERICA.

Published by J. Passmore, 1.. Fleet Lane, Farringdon Street

# RUMBUSTIOUSNESS

Why the boys should drive away
Little sweet maidens from their play,
Or love to banter and fight so well,
That's the thing I never could tell.

James Hogg, 'A Boy's Song'

Generally speaking it is the boys who are the aggressors in the playground. They run through the girls' skipping games, bearing the rope away with cries of 'Tally ho!' They make fun of the singing games, standing at the side of the ring and imitating the girls' actions. (It would be unthinkable for the girls to interfere with the boys' football: they simply withdraw to their own part of the playground, respecting a territorial imperative.) It is the boys, too, who most enjoy the structured violence of Piggyback Fights, Conkers, and the knife-throwing game called Split the Kipper.

In any family of boys and girls it is the boys who carry the guns, and the girls who seek refuge. (The female child in the Opie family was thus persecuted, until provided with a pop-gun.) The assumption that a toy gun or sword or catapult is standard equipment for a boy is centuries old. Children are, after all, being initiated into their roles in life, and little boys grow up to be soldiers and hunters. Pacifist parents may decide to ban guns altogether; but children may still aim a banana at their best friend and say 'Bang, bang!'

Many of the most effective aggressive toys are too insignificant-looking to warrant an appearance in a picture-book, but are remembered by today's adults with abiding satisfaction. Peter Opie was looking round the Liss village toyshop in 1960 when his eye was taken by 'some bombs of the old traditional shape made of lead, the two pieces held together by a bit of string. These cost 4d. The shopkeeper said that they made him feel nostalgic, too, when he first opened the box. They cost a penny when he was a boy more than fifty years ago. He also had plastic ones, price 3d, shaped to look like real bombs, but so far I have not found that these work nearly so well.'

Joke shops are, however, the richest source of legitimized mischief, and in this the grown-ups collude, pretending to be deceived by the box of plastic chocolate creams, to be horrified by the fake dog's mess, to be alarmed by a 'bloody bandage' or a nail apparently piercing a child's finger, and not to have noticed the Whoopee Cushion being slipped on to their chair. It is only fair to allow children sometimes to enjoy the topsy-turvy delights of saturnalia.

There is a wealth of nuisance-value, too, amongst the allegedly musical toys: the bazookas, Swanee Whistles, mouth organs, bird warblers, clackers, Jew's Harps, and humble tissue-papered combs, which, although pleasing to a child's ear, are torture to the rest of the household. The much-respected Pye Henry Chavasse, however, whose *Advice to Mothers on the Management of their Offspring* was first published in 1839 and remained in print for a hundred years, insisted on the child's rights in such matters. 'The nursery is a child's own domain,' he said. 'It is his castle, and he should be Lord Paramount therein. If he choose to blow a whistle, or to spring a rattle, or to make any other hideous noise, which to him is sweet music, he should be allowed, without let or hindrance, to do so. If any members of the family have weak nerves let them keep at a respectful distance.'

The old duelling game of conkers is here represented by (left to right) a 1969 specimen from the majestic horse-chestnut tree at Westerfield, threaded on string; the '2107-er', threaded on a bootlace, which was Conqueror of the 1909 season at Lindisfarne Preparatory School, Blackheath; and a plastic conker, designed to break on contact, which was briefly marketed in 1970 under the title 'Clonkers – conkers all the year round'.

Toy sword of *c*.1820, with fustian-covered scabbard, velvet-covered handle, brass hand-guard and trimmings, and imitation-chased blade.

In Scot's *Discovery of Witchcraft*, 1651 (right) appear pictures of the 'knacks, wherein the simple juggler with words can . . . kill and revive any creature at his pleasure'. Among these is a bodkin with a hollow haft, which appears to pierce the head or the tongue; and, on the opposite page, 'knives of device' that can seem to be 'thrust through your arme, and to cut halfe your nose asunder, &c.' These tricks have been inherited by schoolchildren. The bodkins become trick daggers: examples, top left, from Hong Kong, 1958, and from Germany, *c*.1910. The knives are perpetuated in the well-known 'Magic Nail through Finger Trick'.

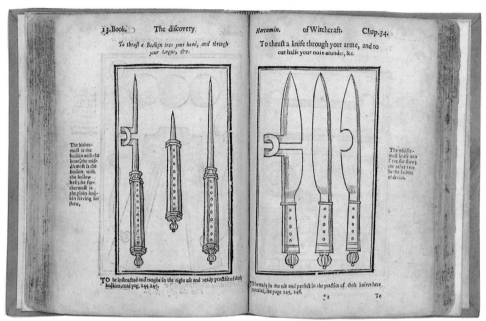

Spoof food of the 1930s. A celluloid broken egg; early plastic fried egg; squeaky rubber bun, apple and orange; joke ice cream wafer ('Harmless, Inedible'), and box of 'chocolates' with a typical 1930s design harking back to the eighteenth century.

Red Indian Shooting Game, made by Chad Valley Games, Harborne, England, c.1935. A plywood Red Indian and his horse are set up at the end of the box, and players, 'standing at an agreed distance', try to hit horse or man with wooden bullets shot from a spring-loaded gun. The game emphasizes the change in mores over the past fifty years.

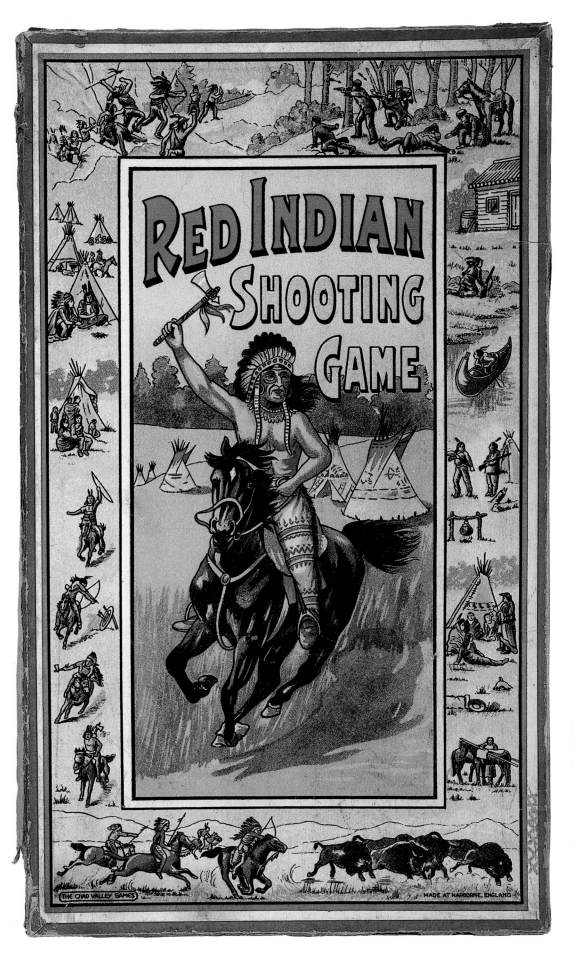

A display of toy pistols, with some percussion caps in the red and green boxes, a coiled 'Revolver Band' of '100 Shots' in the yellowish box, and tiny metal cartridges in the smallest box. Note the ornamental Parisian pea-shooter at the top; the Mexican Repeater pea-shooter, c.1895; the miniature pistol made in Austria, c.1910, which fires blanks with a resounding report; the G-Man Automatic of the 1920s, which fires by clockwork; and the handsome Frontier Sheriff repeater made by Crescent Toys, c.1965 (bottom right).

# MAKING AND DOING

Kiddies and grown-ups too-oo-oo,
If we haven't enough to do-oo-oo,
We get the hump,
Cameelious hump,
The hump that is black and blue!

Rudyard Kipling, *Just-So Stories*

Industry has long been commended as a way of life for the human race, the moralists taking their cue from St Jerome, who, in the late 4th century, gave this advice in a letter: 'Find some work for your hands to do, so that Satan may never find you idle.'

It is entirely true that some of the greatest satisfactions come from making things; and it is also true that for a child to be idle when others are busily employed makes him or her feel unimportant. The Edgeworths understood his plight when they wrote in *Practical Education* (1798), 'Such parents as think of educating their own children, are usually employed some hours in the day in reading, writing, business, or conversation; during those hours children will naturally feel the want of occupation, and will,

from sympathy, from ambition and from impatience of insupportable ennui, desire with anxious faces "to have something to do".' They understood, too, the difficulty of providing children with the materials for making things without at the same time creating an appalling mess for the adults to clear up. 'Those who have never tried the experiment, are astonished to find it such a laborious business as it really is, to find employments for children from three to six years old. Modelling in clay or wax might probably be a useful amusement about this age, if the materials were so prepared, that the children could avoid being every moment troublesome to others whilst they are at work.' How pleased they would have been with Plasticine or Glitterwax!

Parents have reason to be very grateful to the manufacturers of children's amusements, while the manufacturers have, over the past two centuries, known that a ready market exists. The first drawing and painting books were certainly quasi-educational, but they pinned the

Child's scrapbook, *c.*1880, with typical shiny embossed 'scraps' of German manufacture, and a pretty confirmation card made with silvered lace-paper and artificial flowers. The left-hand page of predatory animals shows that Victorian children were not as sentimental as has sometimes been supposed.

The GRAND NATIONAL JUBILEE, August 1st 1814.

A correct view of the revolving TEMPLE of CONCORD as it appear'd in the GREEN PARK on the night of the Grand JUBILEE.

*Convince the World that you are just and true,*
*Be just in all you say, and all you do;*
*Whatever be your birth, you're sure to be,*
*A man of the first magnitude to me.*

The Holy Feast of Easter was enjoin'd,
To bring Christ's Resurrection to our mind;
Rise then from sin, as he did from the grave,
That by his merits he your souls may save.

*Glory to God in the highest, peace*
*on earth, good will toward men.*

The BALLOON ascending with Mr. Sadler Jun.r

Sham Fight on the Serpentine.

Besieging the Castle.

Jubilee Fair in Hyde Park.

The Bridge & Pagoda erected in commemoration of the Peace.

Samuel Unite December 3. 1815.
Aged 13 years.

Printed & Publish'd by LANGLEY & BELCH, 173 Borough, London.

Pictorial writing sheets such as these were filled in by schoolboys when about to come home for the Christmas holidays, to show their progress in handwriting. This sheet was published by Langley & Belch, 173 Borough, London. It depicts the Grand National Jubilee of 1 August 1814. The Prince Regent designed many of the jubilee buildings set up in Green Park, such as the Temple of Concord shown at the top of the sheet, and the Bridge and Pagoda at the bottom. There was a sham fight on the Serpentine; and a mock castle, which was besieged as part of a firework display.

children down as surely as did the later tracing, join-the-dot and magic painting books. Following in Froebel's footsteps, Kindergarten Emporiums produced, in nicely made wooden boxes with elegant labels, a variety of outfits which saved parents and nurses from searching around for the raw materials of useful occupation. Books began to be published which gave instructions for 'things to make and do'. *The Girl's Own Book*, printed in numerous editions from 1837 onwards, tended to concentrate on the making of useful gifts: fancy baskets covered with moss, or alum crystals, or allspice berries; pen-wipers, candle ornaments and pincushions. Soon after the turn of the century, in the wonderful pages of Arthur Mee's *Children's Encyclopaedia*, the emphasis was on gadgets like telephones made from tins and string, and models such as a girl's swing made of spent matches, with lead shot to weight the seat, and an eskimo village with cotton wool snow and igloos of halved eggshells. And ever since the advent of chromo-

lithography and the flood of gloriously coloured paper pleasures from Germany in the late nineteenth century, children have been enjoying the glossy delight of embossed scraps, cut-out books, paper-modelling books, and books with stand-up pictures; as well as boxed occupations with labels alluring enough to inflame any little girl's ambition.

The serious side of occupational instruction had by this time dwindled. After the arrival of the sewing-machine it was no longer strictly necessary to entice girls along the path towards plain sewing by means of the coloured excitements of embroidered caskets and samplers. Early sewing practice has descended to the doubtful artistry of sewing cards; and it needs some guile to persuade small needle-persons that their loosely stitched needle-case is preferable, in granny's eyes, to the more soundly constructed article she sees for sale in Woolworths.

Cabinets such as the above were usually made by schoolgirls to present to their female relations. In the Whitworth Art Gallery is a cabinet made by Hannah Smith, with a note she wrote 'to fortiffi myself, and those that shall enquire about it', recording that when she went to school in Oxford in 1654 she 'made an end of' her cabinet, and that after she came away in 1656, 'when I was almost 12 years of age', the cabinet was made up in London.

The cabinet shown here has been a treasured possession in Peter Opie's family since it was finished in 1668 – and was clearly never used. It is lined with cherry-coloured silk, and contains perfume bottles, a mirror, a trough for pens with pounce-box and sealing-wax dish, and drawers (some of them secret) in which rings and *billets doux* were kept.

The decorations which cover it are either embroidered directly on to the white satin base or employ 'raised work' motifs, which were probably bought from a supplier, leaving the schoolgirl only the pleasant task of appliquéing them in position and concealing the lines of attachment with cord or gimp. Handling these chubby little lions and camels, kingfishers, parrots, and outsize butterflies and caterpillars, must surely have reconciled any little girl to her sewing class.

The front of the box shows Charity, comfortably seated, with a baby in her arms, and a boy and girl by her side. She has given the boy a symbolic heart.

The other sides depict Justice and Prudence, and Temperance and Fortitude; the back has only a floral design, and on top appear Faith and Hope.

Until recent times sewing was for the female sex both a necessity and an accomplishment; and the early 'long' samplers of stitches and patterns served girls as reference works for their future life, as well as proofs of their competence. Over the years the scope of samplers gradually widened to include moral uplift in the form of Biblical texts and sententious verses, and,

finally, some pictorial fun for the young labourer.

Kezia Perrin began her sampler in 1817, and finished it in February 1818. It has all the features common to its period: the alphabet, the numbers up to 100, the stylized house, the flower-patterned border; but surely we may be allowed to believe that Kezia herself is present, and her brother, and their pet dog on its scarlet lead.

The sampler hangs in the Opie dining-room; its colouring tones with the green walls, and its sentiments agree with the Opies' own philosophy:
'Let me O God my labours so employ
That I a Competency may enjoy;
I ask no more than my Life's wants supply,
And leave their due to others when I die.'

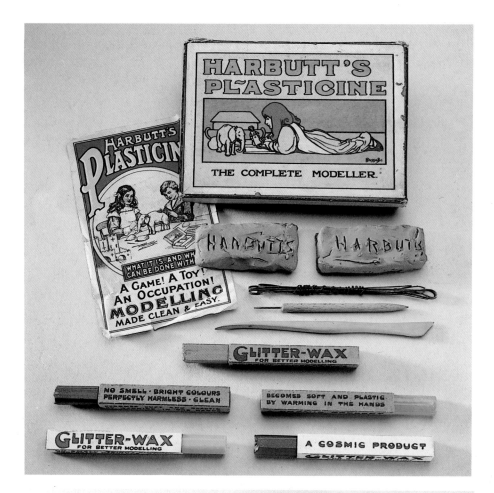

Top: box of 'Harbutt's Plasticine, the Complete Modeller', c.1910, with label by John Hassall, advertisement leaflet, and modelling tools. This patent material brought clean, manageable clay into the nursery, and a ravishing, unforgettable smell.

Below: 'Glitter-wax', c.1925. Before the advent of this famous coloured modelling wax, children broke up coloured tapers with which to model toy food, plates and dishes. In Kingston's *Infant Amusements* an old lady remembers from her childhood c.1835 that 'the wax which became by frequent use too black for these delicate purposes' was converted into kettles, frying-pans, and other kitchen articles.

Boxed occupations of the 1920s: 'Modern Raffia Work' for the creation of mats, boxes with hinged lids, and trays for knick-knacks; 'Wool Winding for Wee Folks', in which small cardboard figures are dressed by winding wool round their bodies; and 'The "Jamboree" Ball Mosaic Game', its shining balls to be arranged in patterns on the perforated black cardboard background.

*My Present for You: a Kinder-garten Painting Book,*
published by Frederick Warne, *c.*1910. This is a compendium
of useful gifts, such as candle shades
and napkin rings, to be coloured, cut out and assembled. It
promotes two of the virtues most desired
in children at that time, industry and generosity.

# FESTIVITY

*Mr Thackeray protests at a recent cartoon by Mr Leech in* Punch, *January 1849:*
'An odious, revolting, and disagreeable practice, sir, ought not to be described in a manner
so atrociously pleasing. The real satirist has no right to lead the public astray
about the Juvenile Fête nuisance, and to describe a child's ball as if it was a sort of
Paradise, and the little imps engaged as happy and pretty as so many cherubs.'

It would be difficult to find many adults who remember the parties of their youth with pleasure. The very circumstances of a children's party spell disaster. A large number of children who do not know each other well, if at all, are penned in a room together for several hours, wearing unfamiliar clothes and simmering with excitement. No wonder the stronger ones dissipate their anxieties by tearing round in circles and screaming, and the weaker ones by sobbing in corners. Their hosts, vaguely aware of the explosive conditions they have created, know their only hope is to plan the party like a military operation, with a master of ceremonies

A page in a *Harrods Fancy Dresses* catalogue of *c.*1920, when so great was the rage for fancy-dress dances for adults or children that Harrods had a special department on the First Floor.

about sandwiches; the game in which she had to run alone into the centre of a circle to catch a spinning trencher, and the embarrassing ritual called 'giving and paying Forfeits'; the game in which she had to file under an arch of raised arms in dread of having her head chopped off – not knowing why this should be, nor why oranges and lemons should be mixed up with talking bells and bedtime candles; the fever-pitch climax when the boys, skidding amongst the debris of spilt jelly and cake crumbs, rolled up the remains of the party streamers and stuffed them down her neck. When rescue came, there was the final worry of shaking hands

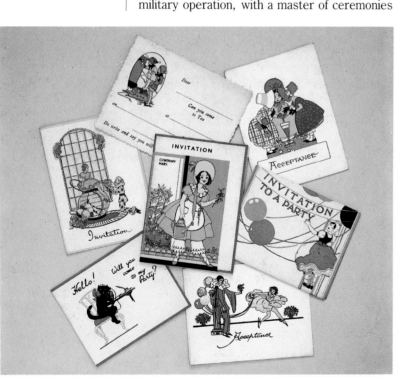

Party invitation and acceptance cards of the 1930s. Social life was certainly made pleasanter for middle-class children when they could choose their own cards to send or reply with – simply filling in names, dates and times was more of a game than a bore.

(ideally a bachelor uncle with a commanding voice), a programme of games and dances, a substantial tea ('That'll keep them busy for at least an hour'), and perhaps the expensive mesmeric services of a party entertainer.

Many a girl has gone home from a party with a burden of horrors in her mind: the memory of the officious talcum-powdered lady who bent over her suffocatingly at tea, with questions

*A Trip to Toy-Town*, a rocker-book published by Raphael Tuck, *c.*1890. Novelty books that were a cross between a book and a toy were produced in large numbers at the end of the nineteenth century.

Party hats and favours, 1910–1930. The chrysanthemum, and the red-faced man, *c.*1910, are both 'blowers' of a superior sort, the tube being decorated along its whole length. In the centre is a tickling stick. The hats are from *c.*1930; and the streamers, made in Japan, *c.*1910, are weighted with wood for greater carrying power.

There were other compensations, of course. Parties often ended with the dancing of Sir Roger de Coverley, with its jolly bouncing tune, its consciously antiquated bowing and curt-seying, and its ingenious progressive movement whereby the couple at the head of the dance was replaced by the next in line. Once (but once seen never forgotten) there was a film of Felix the Cat on a portable screen; 'Felix kept on walking, Kept on walking still,' and his pertinacious plodding was a lasting inspiration. But the real treasures of a party are those one can take home: balloons that had been defended through-out the riotous hours from trampling feet and the envious hands of those whose own balloon had burst; glittering decorations from crackers and their miniature contents, destined for dolls' houses; smoothly coiled paper streamers and fragile blowers and squeakers, smuggled home unbroken; and, from really superior parties, masks, military hats, and funny spectacles and false teeth to transform the face, which would last for years in the dressing-up box.

It may be, however, that the sweetest revenge for having to submit to organized entertainment at other people's parties is when the juvenile host provides the entertainment at his own. There is surely no pleasure equal to running through one's whole repertoire of con-juring tricks, or laboriously putting on stage the resources of one's toy theatre, before an audience bound and gagged by the accepted politenesses of social intercourse.

with the right person and saying, in the approved formula, 'Thank you very much for the nice time.'

And yet, and yet, who can forget the glamour of a rose-pink velvet party cloak with a caressing fur collar, and bronze dancing slippers with pom-poms and crossed elastic? And who will not reminisce about orange jelly in real oranges, made into baskets with angelica stems for handles? And who will not savour the moment at a fancy dress ball when, disguised as the Mad Hatter, she was taken for a boy and invited to join Them?

*The Conjuror – Der Zauberer*, the 'Latest Magic Box', made in Germany, *c.*1910, containing a trick cigarette, ball, coin, and card all 'with preparation for disappearing' (each has the same kind of grip for the middle finger), and a match-box to change into a card.

*Holiday Fun*, in F. Warne & Co.'s Picture Puzzle Toy Book series, *c.*1875. This copy was bought from the Kindergarten Emporium, 57 Berners Street; and certainly a small child could have tremendous fun cutting out figures and presents from the left-hand page and sticking them on to the blanks on the opposite page to complete the picture of the Christmas tree ceremony.

Opposite: In the 1840s Tom Smith had the inspired idea of combining the 'Kiss Motto', a sweetmeat wrapped in fancy paper and accompanied by a love-motto, with the 'Waterloo Cracker', a paper firework device, thus inventing the cracker bon-bon and immeasurably increasing the joys of childhood.

The Edwardian crackers above show how the invention developed. On the box lid of Caley's Japan-British Crackers (bottom left) John Bull is apparently welcoming a Japanese couple to the Olympic Games of 1908, for their luggage is labelled 'White City'. 'The Merry Makers', with two children on the lid quietly feeding a lamb, were 'Specially Manufactured and Shipped for Spencer & Co., Ltd., Madras', presumably to remind Anglo-Indians of their native land. The Brock's 'Crystal Palace' firework crackers are appropriately named 'Fiery Dragon'. None of these crackers has ever been opened, but a motto that has worked its way loose can just be read:
'A kind-hearted fellow called Jinnet,
Fired a Brock's Catherine Wheel and did spin it,
When they saw the cascade of sparks, the kids said,
'Trafalgar Square fountains in't in it.'

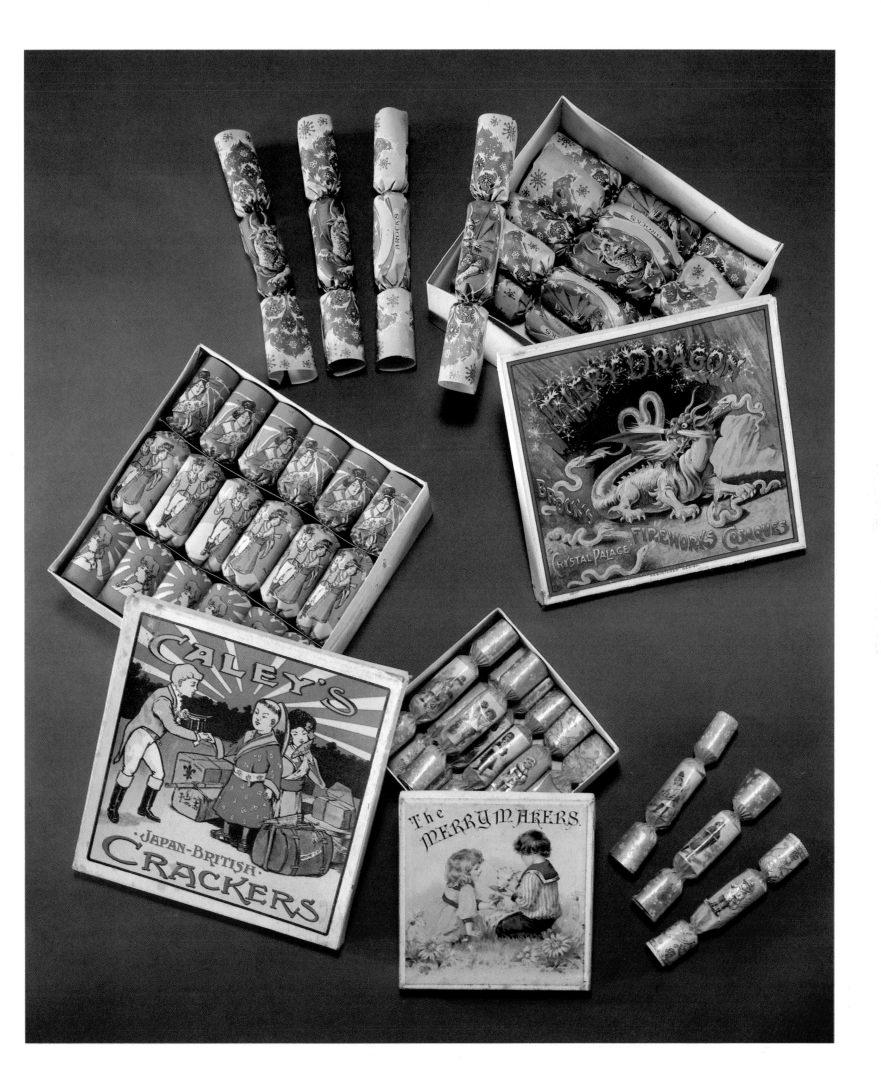

Sophisticated masks of the 1930s, and celluloid and cardboard spectacles and monocle, with facial features attached, from before the First World War. The most spectacular of the ocular disguises is the second up, on the right: when one blows into an aperture behind the black cotton chenille moustache, the eyebrows suddenly shoot up.

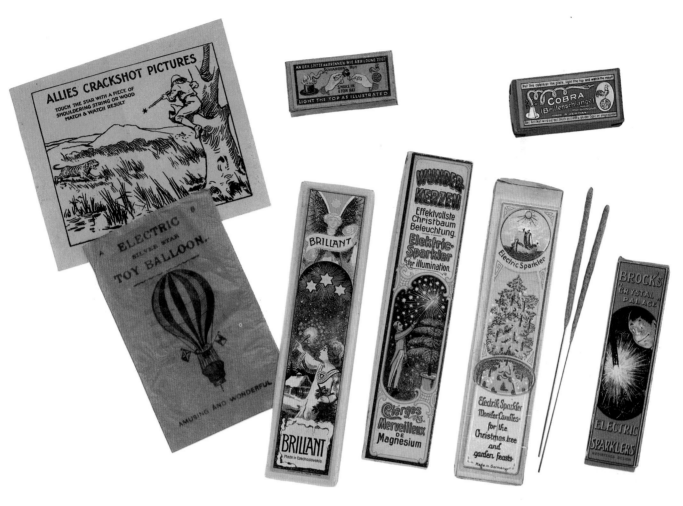

Some indoor fireworks for parties, pre First World War. Top left: one of a series of 'Allies Crackshot Pictures – touch the star with a piece of smouldering string or wood match & watch result'. Bottom left: 'Electric Silver Star Toy Balloon – apply light to top of A and B and watch THE WONDERFUL EFFECT'. Top centre and right: the cone-shaped 'Snake in Eton Hat' and 'Cobra', both of which, when lit, produce long, spongy, snake-like loops. Across the bottom: sparklers made in Germany. The label on the third box, which reads, 'Electric Sparkler Wonder Candles for the Christmas tree and garden feasts', shows that the sparklers were hung upside down on branches and lit from the bottom. At that time 'electric' was used to denote something sensationally bright, rather in the way 'atomic' was used later on.

Peter Pan Bus for Children's Parties, *c.*1955, containing nine gifts for the guests which are distributed according to numbered tickets handed out before the bus is opened, making this a kind of lottery.

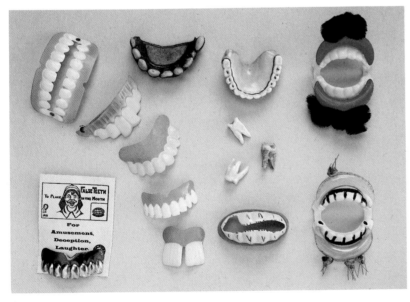

From the Opie collection of 'Disguises: oral', these transfiguring sets of teeth are made of celluloid or china, and date from around 1910. Notice the separate china 'fangs', which can protrude casually through the lips or be brought out of a pocket; and the horrifying celluloid mouth with hairy moles on the lips (bottom right). Adults and children alike enjoyed such gimmicks. Michael Astor recalls, in *Tribal Feeling*, how suddenly burlesque could break out at Cliveden, and that it often started with his mother Nancy, Lady Astor, 'slipping a pair of celluloid false teeth into her mouth in the middle of dinner'.

# BIBLIOGRAPHY

## — WRITINGS BY IONA AND PETER OPIE —

### Books and Articles by Peter Opie alone

*I Want to be a Success.* Michael Joseph, 1939.
*Having Held the Nettle.* Torchstream Books, 1945
   [Stories].
*The Case of Being a Young Man.* Wells, Gardner &
   Co., 1946.
*The Festival of Britain Exhibition of Books.* Cambridge
   University Press, for the National Book League,
   1951.
   Peter Opie was involved with drafting sections on 'A
   Ring of Rhymes', 'A Panoramic Peepshow', 'The
   Child as Author' and 'The Children's Corner', pp.
   22–39.
'The Collection of Folklore in England', paper read to
   the Royal Society of Arts, 25 March 1953.
'Nursery Rhymes', article in Cassell's *Encyclopaedia of
   Literature.* 2 vols., 1953; revised 1972.
'England, the Great Undiscovered' in *Folklore*, 1954,
   pp. 149–64.
'The Present State of Folklore Studies in England' in
   *Folklore*, 1957, pp. 466–71.
'Nursery and Counting-out Rhymes' in *Encyclopaedia
   Britannica*, 1960.
'Nursery Rhymes', Chambers' *Encyclopaedia*, 1961.
'The Tentacles of Tradition', presidential address to
   Anthropological Section of the British Association,
   printed in *The Advancement of Science*, XX, 1963–4,
   pp. 1–10.

### Books, Compilations and Articles by
### Iona and Peter Opie together

*I Saw Esau; traditional rhymes of youth.* Collected by
   Iona and Peter Opie. Williams & Norgate, 1947.
*The Oxford Dictionary of Nursery Rhymes.* Edited by
   Iona and Peter Opie. Oxford, Clarendon Press,
   1951.
*The Oxford Nursery Rhyme Book.* Assembled by Iona
   and Peter Opie; with illustrations by Joan Hassall.
   Oxford, Clarendon Press, 1955.
*Christmas Party Games.* New York, Oxford University
   Press, 1957.
*The Lore and Language of Schoolchildren.* Oxford,
   Clarendon Press, 1959.
*The Puffin Book of Nursery Rhymes.* Gathered by Iona
   and Peter Opie; with illustrations by Pauline Baynes.
   Penguin Books, 1963.

   An edition in hard covers was also published in the

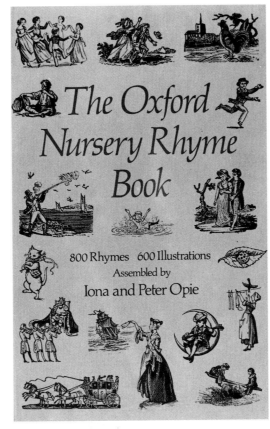

'Proposals for a Dictionary, Arranged on Historical
   Principles, of English Traditional Lore' in *Folklore*,
   1964, pp. 73–90.
'Children's Games and Sports', article in *Encyclopaedia
   Britannica*, 1964; enlarged 1970.
'John Newbery and his Successors' in the *Book
   Collector* 24.2 (Summer, 1975), pp. 259–69.
'The Value of Exhibitions' in *Signal* no. 19 (January,
   1976), pp. 22–6.

United States as *The Family Book of Nursery
   Rhymes.* New York, Oxford University Press, 1964.
*Children's Games in Street and Playground.* Oxford,
   Clarendon Press, 1969.
'Children's Books' in *The New Cambridge Bibliography
   of English Literature.* Vol. II 1660–1800, edited by
   George Watson. Cambridge University Press, 1971.
   Col. 1013–1034.
*The Oxford Book of Children's Verse.* Chosen and
   edited by Iona and Peter Opie. Oxford, Clarendon
   Press, 1973.
*Three Centuries of Nursery Rhymes and Poetry for
   Children; an exhibition.* National Book League,
   1973.

   A 'revised and expanded' edition of this catalogue
   was published in 1977 in a limited edition by Oxford
   University Press in England and by Justin G. Schiller
   Ltd in America.

*The Classic Fairy Tales.* Oxford University Press,
   1974.
'Books that Come to Life' in *The Saturday Book*, ed.
   John Hadfield. Hutchinson, 1975, pp. 61–79.

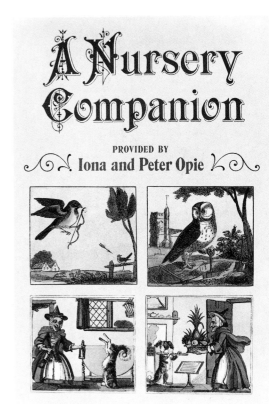

*A Nursery Companion.* Provided by Iona and Peter
   Opie. Oxford University Press, 1980.
'When the Voices of Children are Heard on the Green'
   [discursive interview] in Cott, J. *Pipers at the Gates
   of Dawn.* New York, Random House, 1983.
*The Oxford Book of Narrative Verse.* Oxford University
   Press, 1983.
*The Singing Game.* Oxford University Press, 1985.

Fraser, Antonia. *A History of Toys*. Weidenfeld & Nicolson, 1966

Fritzsch, Karl Ewald, and Bachmann, Manfred. *An Illustrated History of Toys*. Abbey Library, 1966

King, Constance E. *Antique Toys and Dolls*. Studio Vista, 1979.

White, Colin. *The World of the Nursery*. The Herbert Press, 1984. Includes comments on and illustrations from many children's books.

Among more specialized surveys are:

Coleman, Dorothy S., Elizabeth A., and Evelyn J. *The Collector's Encyclopaedia of Dolls*. Hale, 1970 (first published USA 1968).

Greene, Vivien. *English Dolls' Houses of the Eighteenth and Nineteenth Centuries*. Batsford, 1955.

Hannas, Linda. *The English Jigsaw Puzzle 1760–1890*. Wayland, 1972

Speaight, George. *The History of the English Toy Theatre*. Studio Vista, 1969.

Whitehouse, F. R. B. *Table Games of Georgian and Victorian Days*. Garnett, 1951.

Accounts of children's literature are more numerous, but not always more reliable. Perhaps the most penetrating study is:

Darton, F. J. Harvey. *Children's Books in England; five centuries of social life*. 3rd ed. rev. Brian Alderson. Cambridge University Press, 1982 (a book which Peter Opie kept close to his desk, along with Stevenson's *Virginibus Puerisque* and White's *Selborne*).

At a more introductory level may be noted:

Thwaite, Mary F. *From Primer to Pleasure in Reading*. 2nd ed. The Library Association, 1972.

Both of the above books contain substantial bibliographies which will give guidance to more specialized reading.

## Books, Compilations and Articles by Iona Opie alone

*Ditties for the Nursery*. Edited by Iona Opie, illustrated by Monica Walker. Oxford University Press, 1954.

'The Opie Œuvre', *Children's Literature Association Quarterly*, Fall Special Section, 1986.

'Iona Opie, 1923–' in Nakamura, Joyce ed. *Something About the Author. Autobiography Series*. Vol. 6. Detroit, Gale Research Inc., 1988, pp. 203–17.

*Tail Feathers from Mother Goose; The Opie Rhyme Book*. Walker Books, 1988.

This *Nachlass* from work on all the other rhyme books includes pictures or decorations by sixty-two contemporary illustrators. The book was devised and published as a contribution to the Opie Appeal.

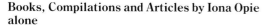

## FURTHER READING

Given the universality of children's toys and games there is a surprising dearth of dependable studies of their history and character (apart from the work of Iona and Peter Opie themselves, which is noted in the previous section). The following general works, however, may provide a helpful introduction:

*Childhood; a loan exhibition of works of art*. Sotheby, 1988. The 968 items in this exhibition included toys, games and *objets* as well as pictures; many books were also lent from the Opie Collection.

# INDEX

—————— ACKNOWLEDGEMENTS ——————

The authors and publishers would like to thank the following
for their kind help in supplying the photographic material reproduced in
*The Treasures of Childhood*:

Angelo Hornak for the original photography of all the toys and games
and most of the books.

Joanna Dodsworth and Clive Hurst at the Bodleian Library, Oxford.

The Robert Harding Picture Library.

Tetsuya Kotani and APT International for the photographs from their
*Mother Goose* exhibition.

Michael Heseltine and Rebecca Seale at Sotheby's.

The directors of Coutts & Company for permission to reproduce
'The Lowther Arcade' on page 119.

Sotheby's for permission to reproduce 'Misses May and
Violet Craik' on page 25.


Brian Alderson writes: First and foremost I must thank my
co-author, Iona Opie, for her enduring patience and hospitality during
the many weeks that I spent among the books at Westerfield.
After the Collection was removed to Oxford I was given much help by
Clive Hurst and Paul Nash of the Department of Special Collections
at the Bodleian Library; and Anne Spence of Richmond, in the North Riding
of Yorkshire, laboured with much diligence to make my draft
manuscript presentable.